Self-e........
Fiction
that sells

Other related titles from How To Books

HOW TO WRITE A CHILDREN'S PICTURE BOOK
and get it published
Andrea Shavick

365 WAYS TO GET YOU WRITING
Daily inspiration and advice for creative writers
Jane Cooper

CHOOSE THE RIGHT WORD
An entertaining and easy-to-use guide to better English
– with 70 test yourself quizzes
Robin Hosie & Vic Mayhew

HOW TO WRITE YOUR FIRST NOVEL
Sophie King

THE FIVE-MINUTE WRITER
Exercise and inspiration in creative writing in five minutes a day
Margret Geraghty

Write or phone for a catalogue to:
How To Books
Spring Hill House
Spring Hill Road
Begbroke
Oxford
OX5 1RX
Tel. 01865 375794

Or email: info@howtobooks.co.uk

Visit our website www.howtobooks.co.uk
to find out more about us and our books.

Like our Facebook page How To Books & Spring Hill

Follow us on Twitter @Howtobooksltd

Read out books online www.howto.co.uk

Self-editing
Fiction
that sells

Discover professional techniques to
improve what you've already written

Lorena Goldsmith

howtobooks

Published by How To Books Ltd,
Spring Hill House, Spring Hill Road,
Begbroke, Oxford OX5 1RX, United Kingdom
Tel: (01865) 375794 Fax: (01865) 379162
info@howtobooks.co.uk
www.howtobooks.co.uk

How To Books greatly reduce the carbon footprint of their books by sourcing their typesetting
and printing in the UK.

British Library Cataloguing in Publication Data.
A catalogue record for this book is available from the British Library.

ISBN 978 1 84528 504 3

Produced for How To Books by Deer Park Productions, Tavistock
Typeset by PDQ Typesetting, Newcastle-under-Lyme, Staffordshire
Printed and bound in Great Britain by Bell & Bain Ltd, Glasgow

NOTE: The material contained in this book is set out in good faith for general guidance and no
liability can be accepted for loss or expense incurred as a result of relying in particular
circumstances on statements made in the book. The laws and regulations are complex and liable
to change, and readers should check the current position with the relevant authorities before
making personal arrangements.

'I believe large numbers of people have at least some talent as writers and storytellers, and that those talents can be strengthened and sharpened.'

Stephen King, *On Writing*

For Robert

Contents

Acknowledgements   **xiii**

Introduction   **1**
    Who is this book for?   2
    What is bad writing?   3
    Entertaining your audience   6
    What is success for a genre book?   7
    No rules, except 'The Rule'   8
    How to use this book   10

1 Getting the plot right   **12**
    How can a plot go wrong?   12

2 Improving the narrative   **26**
    Determining the point of view   26
    Using the right tense   39
    Pacing your story   40
    Creating and placing cliffhangers   44

3 Achieving a good style   49

Telling, not showing   51

Avoiding excessive adverbs and adjectives   64

Revising dialogue: Ockham's razor   68

Resisting the urge to explain: overwriting   74

Being aware of other common style flaws   77

Figures of speech gone wrong   78

4 Perfecting characterisation   80

Choosing the right names   80

Avoiding block characterisation   81

Recognising unempathic characters   85

Avoiding dull characters: John Smith and Jane Roe   86

Discarding 'Random Jim' characters   88

Being aware of stereotypical 'Australian Sheila' characters   90

Developing 'Rigid Jim' characters   91

Dealing with inconsistent characterisation   94

Adding complexity to underdeveloped characters   97

Toning down overdeveloped characters   98

Informing readers about unknown villains   99

5 Crafting memorable scenes and atmosphere   102

How to recognise a poor scene   103

Making appropriate word choices   104

Using unnecessary words   108

Overcoming a lack of dramatic effect   109

Achieving the best setting for your characters   111

6 Elements of copy-editing and basic copy preparation **116**

Understanding the different roles of the development
editor and the copy-editor 117
Understanding and complying with house style 120
Getting to grips with grammar, punctuation, spelling,
clarity and concision 121

7 Getting published **127**

Making an action plan 128
Knowing your readers 131
Getting feedback 135
How to approach a literary agent 135
Approaching independent editors and literary consultants 155
How to handle criticism of your writing 156
Is self-publishing a viable option for you? 157
Conclusion: Self-editing is worth the effort 162

Resources **155**

Index **167**

Acknowledgements

I'd like to thank all my clients at Daniel Goldsmith Associates for allowing me to have what must be one of the most rewarding jobs in the world.

Many thanks go to Jonathan Telfer at *Writing Magazine*, for offering me the opportunity of writing a self-editing series while working on the book, and for his valued feedback.

For support and guidance and for assessing the first draft of this book, I'd like to thank Katie Green, a natural-born editor.

For priceless feedback and constant support, I'd like to thank my close friend, Mina Bryant, a natural-born life coach.

Not last I'd like to thank my family for editing and improving my life every day.

Introduction

Many people have a definite storytelling gift. Over the years of working as an editor and literary consultant, I can pretty much vouch for this. This natural aptitude shows through new and unrefined writing and it's the very place where editors look for great potential in a new writer.

Because you are reading this book, you are likely to be a beginning writer. With this book, my aim is to help you develop this raw potential so you can give your writing the best chance of success *before* it leaves your drawer to go out into the world.

Self-editing Fiction that Sells is a collection of particularly common flaws I have encountered in new writing, as well as a collection of tried and tested suggestions on how to approach them in order to improve the experience your book delivers to your readers. It's not mainly about pleasing literary agents and publishers. It's all about pleasing readers.

After browsing the available literature, courses, workshops, conferences, and podcasts, all aimed at helping writers write better fiction, it becomes obvious that a disproportionate amount of importance is given to *creative writing* in comparison to *self-editing*. Talented English teachers around the world run enthusiastic afterschool clubs on creative writing, but very few have a set schedule for editing and rewriting. Book after book about *what* and *how* to write are being published every year, but this book is not one of them. That's because *Self-editing Fiction that Sells* aims to help you not only to *write* better fiction in the first instance, but to *improve* what you've already written.

Who is this book for?

This book is an informal and highly practical guide to how to develop your novel or short story through editing and rewriting. It aims to act as a useful tool for those writers who have pretty much completed the first draft of their fiction manuscript and are seeking to read it again, at least a few times more, this time in order to apply some structured rewriting and editing. This is what a literary consultant would normally do. A literary consultant's job is to locate specific fragments in a manuscript that need particular development and improvement. To a large extent, self-editing can achieve a similar result and this book, through clear advice and structured exercises, will serve as a tool for you to identify what needs improvement in your own manuscript. It will help you to recognise your own bad writing.

The fiction model used is genre fiction – thrillers, mysteries, romances, or any other type of commercial fiction that involves a protagonist, a protagonist's quest, a conflict and usually a villain – not only because of its popularity with authors and its huge market, but because the main angle in this book will be on the *commercial* aspect of successful writing and publishing.

Self-editing Fiction that Sells doesn't aim to teach fiction editing in general, although hopefully you will develop a keener eye for detail in other writers' work too. Unfortunately, becoming more aware of your own bad writing comes with the risk of becoming more aware of bad writing in general. I'm still not sure this is a genuine advantage long-term.

What is bad writing?

Bad writing is one of those completely unexceptional things with a ninja-level ability to elude any attempt at definition. Very much like the US Supreme Court's 'definition' of pornography, we're not quite sure what it is, but we know it when we see it.

As readers of fiction, we *know* when we encounter bad writing. Sloppy or coarse or clumsy writing seems to make itself obvious in almost any text and it's usually with a great sense of satisfaction that we realise we have become aware of it *and can do better.*

But how about *our own* bad writing? Now this is a different matter. As a literary consultant – and an author myself, albeit of non-fiction – I know one's own shortcomings when it comes to writing don't seem to make themselves obvious at all. After all, my full-time job is to make the author aware of her or his arguably bad writing and advise on achievable improvement. Very often the feedback I get from clients is: 'How come I haven't spotted that?'

Why is it so difficult to spot our own bad writing? It could be because, when you write the very text you're supposed to edit, it's difficult to set yourself in opposition to it. Editing requires a certain mindset, similar to *critical thinking* and opposed to *creative thinking*. While writing, your main concern is keeping the narrative flow going well, not worrying about technical flaws like switches in point of view within the same scene. Note the difference between *creative thinking* mode (narrative flow) and *critical thinking* mode (consistent point of view).

Most writers already possess a natural disposition towards writing. That's how you ever started writing in the first place – it came naturally. So you don't have to develop a creative mindset. It's already there. Writing is one of those hugely powerful interests that many people enjoy. Anyone can see why it's so popular as a hobby. As a passion. Many a time as an obsession. When you write, everything you experience is a resource. Everyday life is a resource for minimalism, such as describing the dishwasher in your mind as you empty it, or describing the way your friend holds her handbag when she gets out of her car during a routine morning in Starbucks. This is *creative thinking* and this is being in that creative mindset that almost all writers share.

On the other hand, *critical thinking* is far from natural. It's something we need to learn and force ourselves to apply to our own thoughts, to the descriptions that came naturally. We can't think critically from a creative mindset. We need to develop a different mindset from which to evaluate our own creativeness. This book will help you gain the critical mindset that all good self-editors share, with tremendous benefits for your creativity.

That's why the best place to start self-editing is when you have a finished first draft. You could of course choose to do both as you go, but writing and editing at the same time is not only distracting and exhausting as far as the creative side is concerned, it can prove highly detrimental too. Constant interruption to revise and edit will damage the fluidity of your writing as an activity and the flow of your narrative.

As a literary consultant, I read unedited fiction on a daily basis. This, over the years, has helped me identify many particularly common shortcomings found in fiction. For the sake of those wary of formulaic fiction, myself included, I will not call them *mistakes*. I will call them *flaws* or *weaknesses*. In the same way, my suggestions will not be based on any *rules* to follow. The old cliché is true, there are no rules in writing good novels – only suggestions based on particular examples. There can only be suggestions, based inductively on particular instances. In the same way a music coach might suggest ending a Key of C piece in the chord of C because it makes it sound 'finished', for example, an editor would suggest ending a particular chapter on a cliffhanger because (a) it creates more suspense, (b) it moves the story forward and escalates the conflict, (c) it opens up further possibilities a few chapters later and (d) it works really well in the context and so on.

By reading *Self-editing Fiction that Sells* and by doing the exercises as you encounter them, you will soon establish an editing and rewriting routine that will help you improve your manuscript to a large extent.

This, however, shouldn't prevent you from seeking a professional editor's help before you publish your book, if you are self-publishing. My strong belief is that self-editing cannot replace editing by a professional editor. A professional editor would give it the necessary 'fresh-eyes view', and assess its market value, as well as ensure standards are met before a copy is ready for print. However, conscious self-editing will considerably improve the quality *and value* of your work.

Entertaining your audience

One of the particularly common assumptions made by new writers of commercial fiction is that they can get away with murder in more than one way. The main assumption is that the readership *won't even notice*. We get this all the time from clients. If the writing flows and the action goes on for page after page after page, that's all that matters and that's all people want in a thriller. 'They're not bothered about fancy stuff like narrative, point of view, style,' we sometimes hear. 'If they are, maybe they should pick Dostoevsky.' 'I'm here to sell, not to win awards,' is one of my all-time favourite defence lines.

The truth is that audiences today are savvier than ever and their unprecedented level of scrutiny shows through in book reviews everywhere. This is true especially for commercial fiction readers. They are increasingly aware of their immense power and influence. If anyone ever doubts this, they should think of the long tradition of writers changing significant aspects of their stories, and even style, to match the audience's expectations. It was unusual when Herman Melville did it over 160 years ago, so Ishmael – with whom the audience developed a deep empathy – survives, but it's common practice now to simply create a survey with clear options, in which authors invite readers to choose between alternative endings to their story. Although I'm certainly not saying this is what you should do.

If a literary fiction author can disregard the expectations of the mass audience – of, say, accessibility and entertainment – that is because they have in mind an equally powerful audience of elite literary critics and award judges. But in our case, your audience is very much aware that the success of your genre fiction book lies solely in sales figures.

The fundamental truth about genre fiction is that it is a form of entertainment. And its audience expects it to deliver just that. Not educate, not influence, not persuade. The reader who invests in your book and spends valuable time reading it seeks to be entertained, so never underestimate your audience and always strive to deliver to the highest of their expectations.

So if you really must make an assumption about your readership, the safe bet is to assume that *all* your readers are editors who earn a living from reading and assessing fiction and perhaps mainly genre fiction. And then go over your work one more time.

This book's aim is to be your editorial aide, guiding you honestly to and through the unconvincing parts of your writing, the fragments that require most of your attention – the fragments that would fail to impress an audience with expectations already in place. This book's main assumption is that you have written or are writing a novel or short story and want to know if you could make it better before you present it to an editor or straight to your readers. In other words, you believe your book might be a good book. But you want to find out if *it could be better.*

What is success for a genre book?

Any survey in the fiction market will reveal that fiction is a pretty crowded place to be in. You have big names, you have no names with staggeringly big sales, you have new names with no sales and no chance of sales.

The more you refine your book, the higher your chances of success.

By success, I don't mean *getting published* alone. Of course, being offered a deal by a traditional publisher is a success in itself.

However, unlike many books on how to improve your writing, here the purpose is not to help you persuade an agent or an editor to take you on, but to *maximise the reading experience your book can offer to the best of its potential.* If you achieve this, agents and publishers will follow. If you decide to self-publish your novel, this book will be of a higher value to you, as it will instil in you an editor's mindset to work from.

For many years, books like this had one goal: to help you get published. Today, getting published is so matter-of-fact, that I (and many others) feel this goal is no longer worthy of much debate or no longer worthy to be a goal at all. If you aim to give *your readers* the greatest reading experience your novel can give, you can't go much wrong with agents and publishers.

So, if you are not being published by a reputable publisher, what is the measure of an author's success? There are three major factors:

1.   sales figures

2.   reader reviews

3.   critical acclaim.

For genre books, this is also the order of their importance.

No rules, except 'The Rule'

If there were any rules in writing fiction, a writer would do well to break them. Formulaic fiction is dull and recognisable and as much fun as *Coronation Street.* Of course, reading creative writing books and taking courses and workshops help a lot. However, none of the principles mentioned there should be taken as *rules* and followed blindly by original and competent writers.

At the same time, going to courses and reading several books on how to write is a golden opportunity for procrastination. That's why I believe a practical self-editing book is more helpful than a creative writing book. In creative writing, you edit generic exercises in order to learn how to edit your own writing, in self-editing, you edit directly your own writing, thus eliminating one intermediary step.

Self-editing is the constructive criticism every writer needs in order to gauge if his or her work needs improvement or not. Without it, there's no other way of knowing whether your manuscript is as good as it can get, unless you involve an independent editor.

Working on my first instalment on self-editing for *Writing Magazine* last year, I realised there is a major difference between creative writing and self-editing. If creative writing works *deductively*, i.e. identifying a universal rule and applying it to the particular instances in your writing, self-editing works *inductively*, i.e. identifying particular instances of previous bad writing and creating principles to apply to your own writing.

For those eager to label this book a manual on how to write formulaic fiction, I'll emphasise that there are no rules here, except one.

Make your readers read your novel or short story until the end.

I'll call this 'The Rule'.

This book is concerned with anything that could break The Rule, undermining your chances to offer a great reading experience.

How to use this book

You can use this book as a weekly programme to edit your entire manuscript and complete one chapter per week. The exercises at the end of every chapter are designed to help you overcome the writer's (or editor's) block and get you at the deep end of your manuscript. Since the exercises are generic and meant to apply to your particular manuscript, there can't be any set beginning. Land where the exercises take you within your manuscript and start revising and rewriting.

I would recommend working through your whole manuscript several times, each time with a particular *filter* in mind. For instance, revise your manuscript once only with consistency of point of view (POV) in mind. Keep strict focus on this alone and don't get side-tracked by anything else. Once you've finished this, start again from page one with showing, not telling in mind and, again, don't get distracted by anything else.

This is the ideal way to start self-editing. After a few times, you will have gained enough skill to start editing in a synergetic way. This is usually a later-stage edit and it could well be the last time you go through your manuscript. The process will feel natural and you will be at ease with editing a fragment for point of view and showing, not telling. This is a firm sign that you have established an editing mindset from which you can work, completely different from the writing mindset, which most writers already developed naturally.

Before you read the first chapter, it would be helpful to have the first draft of your manuscript completed.

Another approach would be to read *Self-editing Fiction that Sells* and make notes as you go and, once completed, start using the notes in your revising.

Self-editing requires commitment and hardheartedness. You need to have a firm excising hand and work with achievable goals in mind. This guide will help you set those very goals – in other words, it will show you what you need to improve at the levels of story, characterisation, narrative, style; it will help you learn how to present your manuscript to the right agents and publishers and gain some market insight along the way too.

I promise you that following the suggestions in this guide will improve your manuscript significantly. I can make such a big promise because I know all my suggestions are market-tested and 'market-approved'. They are based on successful fiction, fiction that sells. Moreover, the guide will also help you to acquire a set of editing skills that will be useful to you in writing better fiction as well as in reading fiction better. Your life as a *reader* of fiction is about to change once you decide to start getting serious about writing it. You might never be able to read for fun again. Instead, you'll be doing research every time you open a book, which in turn will help you to write immensely better.

Every author has a dream reaction from readers for every single scene in their story. Whether it's 'wow' or 'gee', or 'hmm', it doesn't matter, as long as there is a definite reaction that matches the author's expectations. My dream reaction to this book would be 'Aha!'. I'd love to receive *your* reaction at lorena@danielgoldsmith.co.uk.

Now let's improve that manuscript.

Getting the plot right 1

Unlike in literary fiction, where the story is mainly about characters, the story in genre fiction is determined by *plot*. Get the plot wrong and you get the story wrong. Get the story wrong and readers will find it hard or impossible to follow it, which breaks The Rule.

A plot is not a prerequisite when you just start writing your novel; many famous authors admit that writing without a set plot in mind is a liberating approach. However, having a clear idea of what's going to happen will surely help you to avoid a lot of further work and save you thousands of hours of editing once the first draft is completed. Thousands is not an overstatement.

Since this is a book on self-editing, my assumption is that your manuscript is completed in its draft form or at least close to completion and what happens in the story is no longer a vague inkling.

How can a plot go wrong?

In order to establish what can go wrong about a plot, we should first establish what makes a story a good story. Put simply, we all want to read an exciting story and follow an important quest with a strong conclusion. This is common sense for a good reading experience.

How can it go wrong then?

I have put together a list of particularly common shortcomings I have encountered in fiction manuscripts submitted for assessment, each of which makes a plot fail. The most important plot flaws will be dealt with in more detail later.

The conflict is not strong enough

My free local paper could break records in no-story headlines. The last time I opened it, the front-page headline was 'New Home for Abandoned Moggy'. Out of curiosity, I read the first paragraph. A local couple found an abandoned kitten by the Manchester Ship Canal and took it home. A huge photo of the smiling couple holding what looked like a pretty relaxed and happy kitten was next to the headline.

Could you use something like this in a story? Yes, as part of your backstory or characterisation. A character finding a kitten he or she always wanted could add enormously to his or her characterisation, could move the story forward if used effectively (it could be a clue, an alibi, a reason for further development in the story, etc). It would be beyond silly to use it as the main plot in your book though.

Does the protagonist's quest in your synopsis sound strong enough? Is it worth pursuing? Could it change someone's life? The stakes need to be high enough to jeopardise something of extreme value, perhaps someone's life, perhaps humankind. Ask yourself what will happen to the protagonist if he or she doesn't solve the quest. Ask yourself what will happen if the villain gets his or her way. Depending on your answer to these questions, you will know if you have a strong enough premise or not.

The story doesn't suspend disbelief

Suspending disbelief enhances the reading experience, it is an integral part of an immersive experience, so count on this when you make your story extraordinary in every way.

The story doesn't make sense

Even if not everything in your story would make sense in the real world, it *should* in the universe of your story. This is a common flaw in unedited fantasy and sci-fi. Magic or inexplicable happenings in the middle of a techno-thriller set in the future is a common example.

The conflict is not escalated

If the obstacles are easily overcome, the conflict needs to be developed further. If the solution to an obstacle seems too convenient for your protagonist, then it is too convenient for you as the author, this being the surest sign you need to ditch it.

The story is not believable

If your main plot is too far-fetched to convince anyone of its plausibility, it needs changing.

The main plot is delayed unnecessarily

Here you're simply taking too long to introduce the quest into your story. You're concerned with too much scene-setting description or character introduction. For example, don't use a dinner scene if it doesn't add to character development. In fact, please don't use a really long dinner scene at all (unless you're Alan Hollinghurst of course). If you manage to let the readers know the quest in your story by the end of the first chapter, you're pretty much on the safe side.

Plot holes

A loose or weak plot results from plot holes. Sometimes the metaphor is extended when critics refer to plots as being 'watertight'. Here are some examples.

Too many red herrings

This plot hole means cluttering the story with irrelevant details, causing confusion for the reader. This is a particularly common inadequacy in new writing. 'One must not put a loaded rifle on the stage if no one is thinking of firing it' (Anton Chekhov, *Letters to Aleksandr Semenovich Lazarev*). Remember this piece of advice from Chekhov every time you use *any object at all* in your story. Nothing in your story should be random. If it's in the story, readers will expect it to be used at some point later on. That's why writers and literary critics have called this extremely effective plot device *Chekhov's Rifle*, and that's why we'll return to it later on in the book (see pages 22–23). When you read your manuscript again, keep a close eye on any objects being mentioned along the way. Are they used later? If not, exclude them or replace them with something characters can use. In Joanna Price's *Eeny Meeny Miny Moe*, the protagonist goes for a run at sunset with a deodorant can in her pocket, knowing there is a vicious rapist on the loose, targeting local women. She gets back home safely, but the forgotten deodorant can in her pocket plays a major role in the story dénouement. This plot device is valid not only for objects. An event or detail of any type can work just as well, as long as the reader is made aware of it in advance, before it gains any importance at all.

Example

In a science-fiction manuscript we have received for assessment, the protagonist hides from a group of rioters in the ventilation tunnel of a mine. Just when we think he's safe, out of the rioters' sight, the electricity is cut off, stopping the oxygen supply in the ventilation tunnel. This is a superb twist, especially if used as a cliffhanger at the end of the chapter, but it would work even better if readers were made aware of a threat to the electricity supply earlier in the story or if the incident has happened before, during an important event, thus suggesting that there is a problem with the electricity. When it happens again, this time with potentially devastating consequences, it doesn't feel as forced in the story for the sake of suspense.

As an editor, I'm mildly obsessed with randomness. I find details such as '12:43:47' as the time on an email heading in a novel completely annoying. I would appreciate it adds to the realism of the email, but if there is no reason for the time to be exactly 12:43:47 and not one second later, this kind of detail really should not be added in at all. It comes across as childish and attention-seeking for the wrong reasons.

Becoming aware of the potential power every little thing has in your story will help you dispose of any unnecessary objects or scenes that don't move the story forward.

Inconsistencies

Also called 'Homeric nods' (after Horace's annoyance in *The Art of Poetry* at Homer's 'nod offs'), inconsistencies are particularly common plot holes too. For example, a detective who's mentioned briefly as working on the case, when he was known to be on holiday (unintentional 'nod off' on the author's side).

Example

For the last four pages, Jim travels through a third world country. He loves it. He loves the people, the happiness of the children dancing in the street and so on. Four pages later, bang, 'Jim was grateful to have escaped the city and spend some time in the mountains. The air, the bad smells and the general misery around him had almost driven him crazy.'

Deus ex machina

Your characters need a hand from God, fate or coincidence to complete their quest. When you decide to use this device, you accept that your plot can't work on its own, hence it needs rethinking.

Example

Jim the detective meets a psychic who tells him the name of the killer.

A random or matter-of-fact ending

Think about your ending as the conclusion to all your characters' efforts in your story. Would the story end the way it does anyway (i.e. even without the characters' input)? An example would be a detective novel in which the killer is revealed not through the investigation carried out in the story, but by a completely new character who makes a phonecall four pages before the end of the book and tells the police he witnessed the murder and reveals the killer's name and address. A novel's ending needs to be *meaningful* – the ending simply makes sense and we can easily see why it ended in A and not B, C or D – and *satisfying* – we are convinced by the necessity of this ending and can easily anticipate what the characters' lives would be like after the end of the story. Necessity is a powerful attribute endings need to possess. If your story could go on for another 100 pages or, worse, could have ended 100 pages earlier, your ending needs improvement. The more necessary your ending comes across, the more it resonates with the reader's sense of justice.

Loose ends

Think of everything in your book as part of an arc: it starts, it raises and it discharges. This applies to everything, from characters to plot. If a character arc can be perfectly symmetrical or almost linear in a minor character's case, the plot arc would be asymmetrical, with the climax closer to the ending, as in the figure below.

The obstacles are unconvincing

A weak plot is also a plot in which obstacles are either too weak, hence not delivering the expected amount of challenge to the protagonist and entertainment to the reader, or they are removed in an easy and convenient way.

Examples

The villain dies unexpectedly and all is well again, the
villain turns him- or herself in to the police, the police catch
the villain and so on. The most random choice so far for us
was, the villain goes on a cruise around the world and the
protagonist gives up looking for him or her.

The sequel trap

When you intend to write a sequel to your book, you must ensure
you end the story in the first book at the end of the first book.
This means the plot needs to close and the characters *must* solve
the main quest. It's not fair on the readers to ask for their time
for hundreds of pages only to have them find out that they need
to buy the second book to find out how *this* story ends. If you
want a tie-in with the second book, consider adding a minor
background storyline towards the end of the first book and leave it
open, a storyline possibly to become the major storyline/quest in
the second book. A love tension between two major characters that
doesn't completely discharge by the end of the story seems to be a
preferred choice among writers.

Using diary entries instead of escalating conflict

It's beyond the remit of a self-editing guide to discuss plot structure
in general, as a creative writing guide would do. Everyone knows that,
in fiction, stories are based on plots, which means they are structured
in such a way that they start with an exposition, raise the action,
climax and end with a resolution.

American literary agent, Andrea Hurst, summed up what plot is *all*
about: 'To sell your novel in today's commercial world, you really
need a commercial plot. And this means conflict, conflict and more
conflict.' You really don't need to remember much else about plot.

Think of your plot as governed by Newton's third law of motion in classical mechanics: every action has a proportional reaction. (Perhaps it is worth adding that I am interpreting Newton's law and using only the proportionality aspect to illustrate my point.) This means that every single action that takes place in your story must be followed by its own consequences, so a summarisation of your plot would always be in the shape A1 happened, thus A2 happened and *not* diary entries in the shape of, A1 happened *then* B1 happened, *then* C1 happened and so on.

Trey Parker and Matt Stone, the brilliant creators of *South Park* and *The Book of Mormon*, have discussed this during a workshop with students at New York University. You can watch the short video at www.nyti.ms/SW6eMO.

What they're saying in this entirely illuminating lesson is, don't plan out your action linearly: she did this *and then* she did that *and then* she did something else and so on. The more engaging way to do it is, she did this, *but* something happened, so she had to do that (completely unexpected). If you can fit 'and then' within your scene, rewrite it so you can replace it with 'but'.

The temptation to summarise Trey Parker's and Matt Stone's advice in a formula is just too powerful to resist, so here it is:

$$A1 \vDash A2$$

this means that A1 *entails* A2

and never

$$A1 \;\&\; B1 \;\&\; C1 \text{ etc.}$$

This is how great plots are built and, once you become aware of this pattern of action – consequence, action – consequence, strengthening your plot will become a much easier task. Don't fall into the trap of believing that great plots are nothing but raw action packed with episode after episode of heart-stopping danger.

Every time you create an action, you create a desire in your reader that needs to be fulfilled. This means either more *following action* or a *resolution* to the action. The greatest plots are the plots that continuously create and fulfil, create and fulfil, create and fulfil expectations.

Not using plot devices correctly

If you are going to use an everyday object/event/detail in an extraordinary way, make sure you introduce it earlier in the story, when we are not aware of its later major importance. When you finally use it to create a twist in the story, it will feel like the natural course of events rather than like a new circumstance forced in to move the story forward.

Example

Chapter 2: Jim works in a bank as a cashier. He knows that there is a large amount of money in the deposit room, but he doesn't have access to the code to enter the room.

Chapter 3: Jim plans intensely to steal the cash. All the details of the plan are clever and safe. He'll never be caught. There is only one small problem: he still doesn't know the code to the room.

Chapter 4: We learn that, a month earlier, Jim was invited to take part in a training course on dealing with bank robbery incidences, where he would have access to the room on his own for a few minutes. The course will take place in a few days.

What is wrong with this example? The detail of the training session should have been introduced earlier in the story. Because it is introduced *after* we learn about Jim's decision to steal the cash, we feel it is forced in to move the story forward. This creates a feeling of randomness about your story and it comes across as 'not very clever'.

In the same way, don't describe any action that doesn't promise at least a *consequence* later on. For instance, don't say, 'I stood up and went to the bathroom', or, 'I handed the shopkeeper the money and grabbed the shopping bag to leave the shop', if these actions don't deliver consequences directly related to them. Without consequences, actions are no more than paragraph-padding verbosity.

This placement of everyday objects or events within the story has a name. It is called *Chekhov's Rifle*. It is one of the most powerful and efficient plot devices to use in fiction. The device is named after the metaphor of the rifle, used by Anton Chekhov in his letters to his friend Aleksandr Semenovich Lazarev, to describe the principle of *foreshadowing* in drama. Put simply, if a rifle is casually hanging on a background wall in Scene 1, it must be fired in a later scene otherwise it shouldn't be there in the first place. Remember the deodorant can example earlier.

The technique is not restricted to objects only. It can be a minor event placed strategically at an earlier point in the story only to gain major importance later on.

Example

A minor character cuts himself during shaving and wipes his face on a towel in a hotel. Later on, when it turns out he is the killer, his DNA found on the towel confirms the apparently innocent fact that he was in that particular hotel room on a day with no major importance at the time.

Leaving *any* innocent traces along the way is a great way of using *Chekhov's Rifle*.

How can *Chekhov's Rifle* go wrong? The technique loses its effect when it's placed too late in the story. In the above example, the blood on the towel would be placed after we suspect or find out this particular character is the killer, or, generally speaking, when we give the detail of the blood on the towel its true importance. The trick here is to get the reader to treat the detail casually with not much importance.

Red herrings' trap

The trap with using *Chekhov's Rifle* is misleading the reader into thinking that *every* minor event in your story has a meaning. It's similar to the role red herrings play in characterisation. There is an easy way to avoid this trap: avoid using anything random, events or objects, as readers will be at risk of giving them major importance that they will not have in the end.

Remember the action – consequence principle in building your plot. Remember, every time you use a minor object, you create a desire within the reader to see a consequence to it, i.e. either subsequent action or a resolution. Not fulfilling this desire means you will have a failed plot with loose ends, or the start of a mini-plot within your plot and you have never delivered on the promise you have made to the reader.

Example

Jim stepped out into the street without looking back. Behind him, the water tap in the kitchen was still running.

A new chapter of backstory follows immediately after this cliffhanger.

A chapter later:

As he approached his front door, Jim could hear an odd gurgling coming from inside the house. He unlocked the door and pushed it slowly. (*We can almost see the reader wide-eyed waiting for the flood to wash Jim away.*) He noticed with a sense of relief that it was only the kitchen tap running and he turned it off in an instant.

(*The reader, still wide-eyed: 'Are you kidding me?'*)

Exercise

Write a very detailed synopsis of your book (not suitable for agents and publishers, as we'll see at the end of the book). Having a clear outline of events in your book will help you focus better on the quest to be solved. Read your workshop synopsis to a friend and take the 'lazy student test'. The lazy student is the student pestering everyone in the half hour before the exam with the question, 'What happens in this book?' We've all been there. If they're unlucky enough to have, say, Marcel Proust as the topic for the exam, the hard-working students can find themselves a little stuck. But if they have James Patterson, they *can* talk.

The lazy student's reaction to your synopsis can give you *clues* about your story.

✦ 'Is that it?' means your story doesn't suspend disbelief and is too weak.

✦ 'Give me a break!' – not convincing, too far-fetched.

✦ (*Interrupting you in mid-flow and checking watch*), 'OK, so what happens?' – the story is too delayed.

✦ 'Hang on, but you said' – the story is inconsistent.

✦ 'What happened to the detective's father, who was dying in hospital?' – loose ends.

✦ 'The cheat!' – the sequel trap.

2 Improving the narrative

Narrative is what gives literature its uniqueness. It is the voice of the narrator that gives readers that unique insight into characters' minds and souls and forms that special connection no other type of art can form.

In the broadest sense of the word, *narration* means simply *storytelling*. A narrator tells us directly what happens in a story, i.e. a sequence of events (not necessarily consequential) according to a particular perspective or point of view. 'Narration derives from the Latin verb *narrare*, "to tell", and is related to the adjective *gnarus*, "knowing" or "skilled".' (Wikipedia).

Determining the point of view

Point of view (POV), like style and word choices, is one of those vertical aspects of your writing, one that will affect every level of it, from plot, to style, to characterisation. Technically, it forms part of the narrative, because we are told the story from the narrator's perspective.

The point of view in your book will be determined by the relation narrator–character. If the narrator is a first-person voice, it is always related to one (or very rarely more than one, as in Jeffrey Eugenides' *The Virgin Suicides*) character, predominantly the protagonist.

Point of view is a very technical topic in literary criticism and it is beyond the remit of a practical self-editing book to go into too much detail about its technicalities. The **Which Narrator?** section below offers a short introduction to the different types of point of view before approaching the two main problems encountered in fiction writing.

As a literary consultant, I encounter point of view problems in almost every manuscript I receive for assessment. So much so, that my reports now have a permanent section dedicated to it. I usually keep an eye on two types of slips, both of them particularly common shortfalls in new fiction writing.

The first one is *an inconsistent narrator*. The second one is *an inconsistent point of view*.

Which narrator?

Think of point of view as the loop around the reader's neck. You control it. How far and how close do you want to keep your reader to your characters and story?

In classic fiction, and by this I mean 19th and early to mid-20th century fiction, it was common practice to write from a *neutral* perspective. A narrator so detached, it allowed for self-deprecation or sarcasm towards the characters: *'It is a truth universally acknowledged that a single man in possession of a good fortune must be in want of a wife.'*

This is a rare encounter now. The narrator is so closely interconnected with characterisation, that readers have been trained to expect it. I am a big fan of subjective narrators. They give rich insights into characters' personalities and captivating perspectives over events that would otherwise be dumped as mere pieces of information on the reader.

Narrators are *subjective* (the point of view is through a character's eyes), *objective* (the point of view is neutral, not attached to any particular character) or *omniscient* (also called God's eye point of view).

The subjective narrator, in either first or third person, singular or plural, offers a deep, but narrow understanding of the story, whereas the objective narrator, never in the first person, offers a wider, but shallower understanding. That's why subjective narratives are sometimes called *vertical* and objective ones are often called *horizontal*. The omniscient narrator can be as shallow or as deep as the author wants, presenting events taking place miles apart as well as describing deep emotions that characters feel.

Experimenting with point of view

Point of view is one of the most experiment-friendly parts of fiction writing. You can write about anything from anyone's perspective.

You can experiment with a *first-person plural person*, like Jeffrey Eugenides in *The Virgin Suicides*, where the narrator is a group of once teenage boys, now adults:

> *Whenever we saw Mrs Lisbon, we looked in vain for some sign of the beauty that must have been once hers.*

Or with a *second-person narrator* as in Tamar Cohen's *The Mistress's Revenge*:

> *I know you might see this as incendiary, malicious, even creepy. Call it what you will. But, believe me, nothing is further from the truth.*

Second-person narrators used to be a common choice for epistolary novels, and in *The Mistress's Revenge*, the narrative is indeed a long letter sent to a lost lover, but very rarely, the narrator is the reader him- or herself, as in Jay McInerney's *Bright Lights, Big City*:

> *You are not the kind of guy who would be at a place like this at this time of the morning. But here you are, and you cannot say that the terrain is entirely unfamiliar, although the details are fuzzy.*

You can of course experiment with the *unreliable narrator*, as in E.A. Poe's *Berenice*, where we know it was Egaeus, the first person narrator, the one who did it, or as in Chuck Palahniuk's *Fight Club*, where we get to understand that Tyler Durden is nothing more than the creation of the narrator's mind, or, again, as in Tamar Cohen's *The Mistress's Revenge*, where the first-person narrator tries to persuade herself and the reader that she is not losing her mind, although we quite clearly see the opposite. In fact, out of all types of narrators, I think it's the unreliable narrator that pays most respect to the readers and their ability to read beyond the plain. The narrator *relies* on the reader not to trust the story and see that all is not as it seems.

You can even experiment with *meta-narrative*, another laboratory creation of post-modernism, where the identity of the narrator is not revealed until the end or is not revealed at all, as in Benjamin Prado's *Snow is Silent*, where the first-person narrator shows the protagonist trying to work out who killed the victim. We don't find out until the end that the first-person narrator is actually the killer.

However, most writers will stick to the traditional choice of either first- or third-person narrative and the question is which one should *you* choose.

When you try to decide which narrator is for you, ask yourself whether you want *intimacy* or *perspective* for your readers.

The first-person narrator

A first-person narrator is the ultimate subjective narrator. It cannot narrate anything it cannot witness under normal circumstances.

It would be odd for Hannah to lie in her bed and think, *'Jim felt his fear of spiders was too much to bear,'* when Jim sees a spider in his bedroom, 60 miles away from Hannah's.

There are exceptions. Markus Zusak wrote *The Book Thief* from the first-person perspective of Death and Alice Sebold wrote *The Lovely Bones* using a first-person narration from the point of view of a young girl, who, having been murdered, watches her old world from heaven and is able to describe all the characters' feelings and thoughts.

One of the advantages of a first-person narrator is that it lets your character's personality shine through better than any other narrator. It gives the character intimacy and a huge amount of vividness.

That's why first-person narrators work so well for the chick-lit genre as well as the horror genre.

Some critics argue that a first-person narrator dilutes suspense rather than enhancing it, because we know what the narrator knows – after all that's how we get to know everything in the story. Many others and I disagree. The unreliable narrator (as we have seen in *Fight Club* or *Snow is Silent*) is just one of the great inventions to get around this mere hiccup.

In a multi-location thriller, a first-person point of view would be quite restrictive, so you would have to consider multiple narrators and alternate their stories. But in a horror or psychological thriller, a first-person narrator can offer rich insights into characters' minds that an objective narrator wouldn't normally have access to.

The third-person narrator

If the narrator is a third-person voice, it can be either a character or a stand-alone voice, sometimes mistakenly called *the author's voice*. The narrator can't possibly be the author for one main reason, i.e. the author is a living person and the narrator is a fictional voice.

And this brings us to the first most common shortcoming in point-of-view writing.

The inconsistent narrator

When Emma Donoghue chose to narrate *Room* from five-year-old Jack's perspective, she made a commitment to narrate the whole story in Jack's language, even though the perspective is incredibly restricted: a five-year-old child who lived all his life in an 11ft square room and thinks that anything outside this room is outer space. Despite this, the narrator kept a hugely consistent voice. I can only imagine how hard it must have been to make sure that every reference Jack made or every word in the way he told his story was consistent with his age and condition.

Your subjective narrator *must* narrate through your character's voice, with its own weaknesses and idiosyncrasies.

If your point-of-view character is a car mechanic, very controlling, obsessed with perfection and thinks no women could ever compare to his mother, the way the narrator presents the story must follow all these features.

This becomes crucial if you use alternating points of view. If you have two point-of-view characters and you alternate their episodes, you have made a commitment to follow two different voices, consistent with their respective characters. A neutral voice, which they can both use, would be a disaster not only for your narrative, but for your characterisation too. Matching language, accent and word choices, mood, attitude, tone, purpose and so on is not a matter of choice.

The inconsistent point of view

By far the commonest shortcoming in handling point of view is the confusion *observation–perception*. Observation is commonly confused with perception and vice versa and this results in an inconsistent point of view.

What's wrong with the point of view in this example extracted from a submission?

> *Intending to notice who was working and who was wasting time, Sir Rupert was walking steadily along the rows of men and older boys, of whom there were about 80, amongst them, Mr Inkpen, whose right arm, more accustomed to lifting an ale glass, felt as though it was filled with lead.*

That's right, the point of view jumps from Sir Rupert's perspective to Mr Inkpen's. Sir Rupert can only *observe* how Mr Inkpen is working, not *perceive* how his arm felt. How would you edit this to keep the message as close to author's style and language and keep a consistent point of view?

I chose to replace 'felt' with 'moved', so it reads '(...) *whose right arm, more accustomed to lifting an ale glass, moved as though it was filled with lead*', which is how it appears in the published version (Alan Watts, *Touched by Angels*).

A frequent instance of the confusion between observation and perception is a combination of facial expressions and inner perceptions.

Example

He eased his body in the chair, the pain still crushing his chest, a painful grimace on his face.

A narrator that can see a character's grimace cannot also feel his chest pain, so it's an inconsistency a careful self-editor would pick up.

Although some editors believe there's nothing wrong with changing point of view within the same scene, such as Alicia Rasley in *The Power of Point of View*, many more, including myself, believe it's better to keep a single point of view per scene to avoid confusion.

Why? First of all, jumping from head to head confuses and tires the reader and can make your characterisation efforts gain Herculean proportions. Even paying extra attention while editing, at the end of a 'jumpy' scene, I find it hard to attribute certain perceptions to the right characters, which doesn't help me make my mind up about characters as a reader. If there is one thing writers fear, it is to be misunderstood. I strongly believe that using multiple points of view within the same scene will lead to misunderstanding and confusion.

How do you deal with this when you're at the editing stage? Of course you could rewrite the scene. You could rewrite entire fragments so scenes have one point of view each.

But you could also split them up and use a blank line or a '***', as in this anonymous example based on a submission:

> 'What about me?' wailed Hannah. She couldn't believe her ears. Jim simply didn't seem to care one jot about her.
>
> 'The snake won't hurt you, he's only a baby!' said Jim following her with a dejected look in his eyes. She really looked scared. Could she be so scared by a baby snake? This was just ridiculous.

Again, the same confusion and jump from one character's head to another. You could rewrite the scene, so it's all Hannah's point of view or all Jim's point of view, or you could split it up as in this example:

> 'What about me?' wailed Hannah. She couldn't believe her ears. Jim simply didn't seem to care one jot about her.
>
> 'The snake won't hurt you, he's only a baby!' said Jim following her with a dejected look in his eyes.
>
> ***
>
> She really looked scared. Could she be so scared by a baby snake? This was just ridiculous.

One of my favourite examples of slipping narrators, which is just a pleasure to pick on, is when the point-of-view character is simply not present at a scene taking place.

Example
Hannah felt the hot bubbles relieving the stress in her shoulders, unaware that at the same time, Jim was being taken hostage in the middle of the Nevada desert.

This is a classic mistake, especially encountered in old-fashioned detective stories, in which characters go about their business 'unaware they are being watched'.

Authors who write incessantly in an inconsistent point of view have highly visual stories, where the perspective focuses on different characters from cut to cut, with the addition that in literature, we are often told what different characters see, feel, think, experience.

In film, point of view has a slightly different meaning than in literature. It means mainly the subjective perspective of a character, i.e. we are given the character's perspective to experience the scene as the character would experience it through his own eyes. For this reason mainly, the point of view in film is also called *optical affiliation*. Very effective in horror (and pornographic) cinematography, this point-of-view shot is now very rarely used.

Exercise

Spot what's wrong with point of view in the following fictitious examples, based on real writing:

1. As the second shot reverberated through the forest, a few fellows started running towards the wretched body, now lying in a pool of blood. As others congratulated the marksman, a shaken Jim and Adam stepped gingerly over the stained grass and approached the man, who, by accent, appeared to be Scottish, with their own congratulations. Just as Jim, looking at the hunter wide-eyed, grasped that the man is not unknown to him, Adam felt terrified by his own reaction to seeing his first wild boar a few feet away from him, even though dead.

Would you be able to remember a few pages later who grasped that the man wasn't unknown to him without rereading the paragraph? Can you remember now? Was it Jim or Adam? Try and rewrite the paragraph and change to a single point of view.

2. Can you spot any point-of-view inconsistencies below? How would you fix them?

Hannah stares ahead, fear pressing over her heart like a hot stone, eyes sparkling wildly in the night, unable to see that the ship is descending straight towards her. Two more minutes and she'll be hit. She turns around and starts running as fast as she can. Too late.

Avoiding inconsistency between narrator and dialogue

It's easy to transfer point of view and create an inconsistency while writing dialogue. Let's use the same example.

Example

'What about me?' wailed Hannah. She couldn't believe her ears. Jim simply didn't seem to care one jot about her.

'The snake won't hurt you, he's only a baby!' said Jim looking at her with a dejected look in his eyes.

She looked exhausted.

What happens here is again the narrative point of view being transferred from one character to another, this time in dialogue. The dialogue was in Hannah's point of view at first, because it presents her thoughts and feelings, '*She couldn't believe her ears. Jim simply didn't seem to care one jot about her*' and what she sees and experiences, '*said Jim looking at her with a dejected look in his eyes*'. So far the point of view is consistent. However, by adding, '*She looked exhausted*', the author switches the perspective to Jim's character, to what he sees and experiences.

This switch is common in writers of highly visual scenes, which are built as if watched in a film, with the camera switching from Cut A to Cut B, back to Cut A and so on and dialogue seems to be just that, an exchange between A and B.

Point-of-view consistency can easily turn into a nightmare for any editor, so make sure you revise every dialogue scene before you submit it to an agent or editor.

'Showing, not telling' characters through the narrator

A particularly common failing in constructing a convincing narrative is when the narrator is so eager to make sure we grow the right feelings towards certain characters, that it simply *tells* us, instead of giving us the right clues so we can make our own mind up. (See Chapter 3, *Achieving a Good Style: Telling, not Showing*, on page 51.)

Example

Hannah was very tired at the time, so understandably she made a mistake.

Obviously, Jim wasn't there, so he had no clue what she was talking about.

Hannah had enough of being told off, that's why she's decided to stand up for herself.

Hannah had gorgeous blue eyes.

Jim was a good-looking lad too.

Hannah frowned and told him to go in an unfriendly manner.

Sometimes, this narrative flaw can go to surprising lengths, such as adding brackets within the narrative, where the narrator tells the readers exactly what they should understand, as opposed to what the characters would mislead us to understand.

Example

'Jim sensed (correctly) that Hannah was a little wary of him. He told her he would be back in a few days (he had no intention of doing so).'

Adding 'correctly' and 'he had no intention of doing so' is plain *telling, not showing* and it doesn't allow the readers to immerse themselves into the narrative of your book – it takes the experience away by telling them plainly what to understand from the story. Instead, the hypothetical author of this life-based example could consider adding a line in which to show Hannah being wary of Jim – perhaps something she says, the way she says it, her use of words, a facial expression, a body language sign – anything that would allow the reader to understand Hannah's wariness of Jim. As a safety choice, try to avoid using brackets in fiction, because in non-fiction they are an explanatory emblem.

Using the right tense

There is one easy way of getting the tense right in your novel: keep it consistent. Even easier, stick to one version of it. For thriller novels, the safe bet is always the past. If you have your action take place now, it adds to the complexity of the story and, as with all systems too complex, the likelihood that something might go wrong at some point is higher.

As with point of view, the way you use tense will give you control over the way your readers experience your story. You want intimacy? Use the present tense and first-person narrator. You want perspective? Use third-person and past.

Good tense is an easy achievement if you stick to one version of it. The good news is that it is easy to spot, as it seems to stand out, as shown below.

Example

Hannah gets off the bus and stepped onto the pavement in front of the new estate. 'The bushes go a long way back. I like that,' she thought. She realises at once she finally found something worth looking at.

Pacing your story

A good thriller will alternate action with description and reflection. Political or social thrillers (the 'thought-provoking' ones) will use more of the latter than an explosive anti-terrorist military thriller will. Techno-thrillers will use more of the description technique, to familiarise readers with completely unfamiliar gadgets.

Whichever way you decide to tip the balance, a mix of the three is ideal. For this, you can use the *pace* to speed up and slow down your story. If, after pages of heavy-handed action, readers feel the experience is getting too intense even for the liking of veteran thriller junkies, it's ideal to cool it down with a description of the setting or with a short reflective episode from the protagonist on what to do next.

Dealing with saggy middles

Middles can be drawn out affairs. They never seem to deliver quite the excitement of beginnings or the satisfaction of endings. Characters don't appear to achieve anything and the story struggles to get anywhere.

This is particularly the case with novels written without a clear plot in mind. You know how to start it all, you know the ending, even the climax is crystal clear, but what happens in the middle is a bit blurry. A long car drive, a long walk in the park, a never-ending conversation over dinner. It seems to go on a bit and at some point you breathe in relief that the climax is approaching and the ending will shortly follow.

There are some tested and proven ways to deal with saggy middles.

1. Call in backstory. One of the great ways to push your middle up a notch is by using the backstory. This is why a compelling backstory is so important in a thriller. You can rely on it to create a variation when your main story sags a little. So make sure you plan out a parallel plot for your backstory and the beginning, middle, climax and ending are not overlapping, but rather arranged in an alternating pattern, similar to a lattice. A twist in the protagonist's personal life is a good example. Her mum was taken to hospital (*Chekhov's Rifle* opportunity flags up here, make sure you mention her mum's health problems *earlier* in the story, before they are needed) or she meets someone she falls for completely (make sure this would work with your audience).

2. Escalate the conflict even more. Increase the stakes by adding even more obstacles in the protagonist's way. James Patterson is the master of all second-paragraph twists. If something unexpected happens and ups the stakes of the whole quest, this is great conflict escalation. On a smaller scale, think of mini-conflicts you could escalate: does your protagonist have any phobias? Make sure he or she overcomes the mother of all encounters with the biggest subject of their phobia. No reader is going to put your book down when, while opening a bag of rice, your protagonist, a well-known to readers arachnophobe, finds a scorpion inside. A *living* scorpion. No reader is going to put your book down when your protagonist, a long-time sufferer of asthma, drops her inhaler through the drain grid inside a smoky and dusty mine. In the same way, you can reveal a secret with devastating consequences for the protagonist, which he obviously overcomes in ways unexpected by the reader.

3. Keep alternating. What quite a few writers submitting manuscripts for assessment to our consultancy do is use a vast part of the middle of their book for 'character development'. This sounds like a good excuse, except that characterisation should be done organically and throughout the book, not in a block at the start of your book *or* in the middle. Character development here often means bogging your protagonist down with endless inner monologue and moral dilemmas over completely everyday things (like recycling vs. dumping). While a good old inner conflict can't do any harm, when revising your ms, pay particular attention to whether action alternates with description and reflection just like in the rest of your book. If it doesn't, make sure you see to it. Reflection scenes are scenes in which nothing happens. They are there to develop character, add depth to narrative and maybe create further suspense and conflict. Use reflection to *delay* suspense, but never to *end* it.

Example of bad usage of reflection

Hannah stopped breathing when she realised the revolver was pointing at her forehead.

This could be a good cliffhanger, but completely wasted if you start the next paragraph or chapter with:

Thinking about it now, while watching the clock on the
Mayor's Dome, from her seventeenth floor window, that was
a close encounter. That revolver could have easily had six
rounds instead of five.

Contrary to popular belief, saggy middles are only easy to spot in
another author's book, but not in our own. Just like bad writing
in general. I once heard an editor saying, 'If the author gets bored
while rereading, imagine what a paying reader will be like.' But
this is the trap: the author *never* gets bored. The author knows the
focus and the perspective and where the story will head and he or
she also knows that there is a good reason why that fragment is in
a particular place. In informal conversations about manuscripts,
I've never seen a greater speed of reaction than a writer defending
his or her own choices. It almost defies the laws of physics.

Recognising and improving bad pace

A bad pace is not an inconsistent pace. There is no such thing as an
inconsistent pace, as a pace gets better the more inconsistent, pattern-
resistent and scene- or character-suitable it is.

A bad pace is an *unbalanced* pace.

Example

You build a long dialogue scene in which Hannah and Jim
are trying to translate the coded message received from
space. They try various patterns, but nothing works.

At the end of the five-page long dialogue, we read, 'They
did everything they could and around five a.m., they finally
deciphered the code. They could now move on and start on
the transmission of the message to the Lunar base.'

Painstakingly slow for five pages, in which we have to follow the dialogue lines of Hannah and Jim, even the author has had enough and rushes to the dénouement of the scene.

Slowing down the pace to give the reader chance to breathe is a really good idea, but it must not feel forced into the story for the sake of it.

After a thunderous scene in which Jim nearly got killed in every second paragraph, we move into Hannah's bedroom.

Example

Hannah was sitting on the couch when her mobile started to buzz in her handbag. She got up and walked slowly to the other side of the room, where her handbag was, on top of the sideboard.

She had to look around in her bag for a few seconds before she found it.

'Hello?' she said after she flipped it open. 'Jim?'

By the time we reached 'Jim', we can pretty much see the readers' eyes either rolling or closing.

Creating and placing cliffhangers

At Daniel Goldsmith Associates, we conducted an informal survey in which we invited readers of fiction to answer a few basic questions about their reading habits. One of the questions was, 'When interrupting or abandoning reading, do you usually aim to reach a natural break in the story (e.g. the end of a chapter)?' In response 81% said yes. We read in chapters. Usually it's one, two, three or more chapters per sitting. The natural conclusion then is, the more grabbing the end of a chapter is, the more likely we are to continue through to the next chapter without interruption. Best-selling mysteries and thrillers seem to grab the readers' interest in such a way that they, of course, 'cannot be put down'.

Cliffhangers are a by-product of serialisation in newspapers and magazines. At the end of each episode, authors such as Thomas Hardy would add a cliffhanger in the hope that readers would feel engaged enough to buy the next issue. Cliffhangers were added as an extra, they were mainly conversational (the author would add an extra bit of dialogue and end it with a question) and understandably, the practice came across as rather manufactured and forced-in for the sake of selling the newspaper. That's why, in the full version of the novel, these cliffhangers were often left out.

In time though, cliffhangers became an elaborate and very effective technique for constructing a compelling narrative, engaging the readers and moving the story forward. I can't even imagine now reading a thriller or mystery without at least a few cliffhangers in the right places.

What's in the anatomy of a cliffhanger? *Anticipation* and *build-up* are part of a good cliffhanger and, for maximum effect, the tension never discharges immediately. Cliffhangers work well at the end of chapter or, in the case of a multi-layered plot, at the end of a section followed by a change in plot layer.

I have found that some writers achieve a very effective way of grabbing a reader by the throat by breaking the narrative flow mid-scene, creating a cliffhanger, starting a new chapter with a minor backstory event and discharging the cliffhanger scene ideally mid-chapter, *not* at the beginning of a new chapter.

In thrillers that have an extremely fast pace, James Patterson style, you can comfortably create a cliffhanger at the end of every chapter and discharge the tension at the very beginning of the following chapter, because very shortly after, you will be starting to build up towards another cliffhanger and so on. This technique seems to create the famous 'page-turner effect' most effectively.

Be careful, because in building an effective cliffhanger, you could fall into traps you have set up for yourself, as in this example mentioned earlier:

> After a huge struggle with the militia, Jim manages to hide inside the ventilation tunnel of a mine. Suddenly the electricity is cut off and the ventilation stops, ending the oxygen supply for Jim.

If there was a short mention of the militia threatening to stop the electricity supply in the mine when the detail bore no importance (see *Chekhov's Rifle* in *Not using plot devices correctly* on page 21), this is a great cliffhanger and it works brilliantly, as it will form a workable twist – *unpredictable, yet explicable*. But if the militia *accidently* cut the electricity just for the sake of a cliffhanger, the trick fails. In this example, based on real writing, the author has created a cliffhanger, but he missed the opportunity to extract the most potential from his existing material. That's where an editor would prove helpful.

Mid-chapter cliffhangers

If you have a *multi-plot* novel (i.e. a novel with a main plot and a backstory) or a *multi-layered plot* (i.e. different characters pursuing different threads, but converging around the same quest), mid-chapter breaks can work especially well in building suspense, engaging the reader and moving the story forward.

The breaks are usually signified by '*' or '***' and they show a change in setting or at least point of view – it could be the same scene, but changing the narrators or character's perspective.

Exercise

Open your manuscript and go to the end of your first chapter. Is there a cliffhanger? If not, consider breaking the chapter earlier in the middle of a tense scene. If there are no such scenes, it's back to rewriting time. Consider rewriting the chapter ending or rewrite a mid-chapter scene that could work well if it is broken up. Repeat the exercise with the following chapters, except for the last one.

Achieving a good style **3**

The contemporary American painter, Jasper Johns, once said, 'I feel that works of art are an opportunity for people to construct meaning, so I don't usually tell what they mean. It conveys to people that they have to participate.'

This is the whole point of art in general: participation. Interaction. Suggesting a meaning in your message and inviting the receiver to add to it.

Fiction is certainly no exception. Because it uses written words to convey a message, and not more abstract media such as sound or shape and colour, it's easy to just *tell* the reader what you mean. What he or she should understand. In all my years of working with authors, I can promise you that, for any writer, no fear is greater than the fear of being misunderstood.

Style in fiction is the way in which a message is written. Ideally, it should be of some artistic value. And exactly here is where the number one flaw in beginning fiction writing is committed.

Telling, not showing is a major shortcoming in unpublished fiction writing, hence the disproportionate importance it gains in this book.

In his essay, *Politics and the English Language*, published in an anthology in 1946, George Orwell has some good style advice for authors.

1.   *Never use a metaphor, simile, or other figure of speech that you are used to seeing in print.*

2.   *Never use a long word where a short one will do.*

3.   *If it is possible to cut a word out, always cut it out.*

4.   *Never use the passive where you can use the active.*

5.   *Never use a foreign phrase, a scientific word or a jargon word if you can think of an everyday English equivalent.*

6.   *Break any of these rules sooner than say anything outright barbarous.*

Half a century later, they still stand.

A common style flaw

A common finding in unedited fiction is the repetition of the same connector, giving your writing an unattractive, long aspect.

Example

The group that was formed by pupils and teachers walked
into a small empty room that had a dwarf-size door that
was leading to the spiral stairs that were made of stone.

How would you edit this fragment? The poor quality of writing
thankfully doesn't matter here and no, the example was not
exaggerated for the sake of the demonstration. It is based on a real
extract from a fantasy manuscript. The first step would be looking to
see if you could ditch some of the annoying *that*s.

> The teachers' and pupils' group walked into a small, empty
> room with the dwarf-size door leading to the spiral stone
> stairs.

Once the style has been dealt with, spend a few more minutes on
the fragment looking at its narrative. Who's speaking? Is it the
teachers' and pupils' perspective? If so, how would they know the
dwarf-size door leads to the stairs described in detail by two
attributes (*stone* and *spiral*)? If it's their perspective, unless the
door was open, they would have no way of knowing and you end
up with an inconsistent point of view.

Telling, not showing

What's wrong with this?

> 'Jim felt hurt that his wife did not discuss her plans with
> him'

I hope you would agree that it would fit more suitably in a
psychological report than in a sci-fi thriller.

The temptation to spoon-feed the reader about your characters' thoughts, emotions or *real* intentions is hard to resist. It's wired deeply into our minds not to go around in circles if we can go in a straight line. It's how we think and speak every day. Summarisation is what we are encouraged to do for the whole length of our school years. Remember? Read the text, write the summary, read the text, write the summary. Clarity and concision are skills teachers ensure are drilled into the way children will communicate as adults. When we want to make ourselves understood, we try our best to be clear. And there's nothing a writer desires more than his message to be understood by his readers. So be reassured that summarisation is a skill your readers are very likely to possess by the time they read your book. As they finish reading your book, they should be able to summarise your story without actually quoting it from the book.

Besides, there is also that nagging awareness that, once our book is out there in the world, it starts living a life of its own. We simply don't get a second chance to *explain* what we meant and knowing this can easily turn us into obsession-driven, precision pursuers.

So why on Earth would we show Jim starring blankly at his cup of coffee, just after a row with his wife over her plans? Why would we trust the reader to get the message, when we can ensure they get it by stating it loudly and clearly? *He felt hurt.* Period.

One of the answers would be that it requires more effort. We would have to build a scene to show Jim's sadness. We would have to worry about its atmosphere: is it atmospheric enough? Is it too much? On top of it all, it might mess up our characterisation – after all, it's not like Jim to get all sad and melancholy over a row – so we might have to go back over the whole thing and do a lot of rewriting that we wouldn't have to do if we just went for the, 'Jim felt hurt that his wife didn't discuss his plans with him.' Simply stating Jim's sadness is no less, on the micro scale of this detail, than saying 'Jim couldn't have been there on the night of Hannah's murder, because he was on business some four thousand miles away' on the scale of the major plot.

Fiction works well as a form of escapism and we read books because we want to get involved in an extraordinary and enthralling story and empathise with characters. In a few words, we want to compensate for the lack of drama in our lives. As a writer, you achieve a dramatic effect and give your readers the experience they seek by *showing, not telling*. This is by far the number one flaw in fiction writing, hence the disproportionate emphasis I put on it throughout the whole length of this book.

There is a safe principle of avoiding telling: try to avoid abstractions, such as **emotions**, like *sad, happy, delighted*; **states of mind**, like *scared, nervous, ready for it*; **attitudes** like *angry, argumentative* or **moods**, like *melancholy, emotional*.

Example
Jim felt nervous.

Here, instead of this, you can show Jim biting his nails, clicking his knuckles, biting his lips while narrowing his eyes.

Dangerous abstractions are also nouns like *love, hate, tenderness, tension, intimacy, weakness, satisfaction* and so on.

Example

He felt the love and tenderness embracing him.

Anger was building up inside her at the speed of light.

She knew all his weaknesses.

Strunk and White, in *Elements of Style* had a principle to avoid this:

> *Prefer the specific to the general. The definite to the vague,*
> *the concrete to the abstract.*

It's also safe to stop your narrator from *explaining* a character's real intentions or feelings, another commonly encountered flaw in new writing.

Example

She sank back in her chair. This was so not how she envisaged it all.

Instead of making such a plain and summarised statement, consider stopping at 'She sank back in her chair and rested her head on her hands'. Remember: don't *tell* feelings, show visual expressions. Don't *tell* atmosphere, create a word picture.

A word picture is a visual description of your scene. Instead of saying 'Hannah was exhausted', say 'The circles under her eyes looked deeper than ever'. A word picture doesn't have to use only visual references. In fact, any picture that addresses the reader's senses rather than his intellect is a word picture. Notice the difference, *The carriage went down the gravel country lane* and *The carriage crunched its way down the gravel country lane. The film ended* as opposed to *The lights came on.*

As you read through your scenes, keep a visual filter in mind and always remember Chekhov's famous piece of advice: 'Don't tell me the moon is shining; show me the glint of light on broken glass.' Can readers *envisage* your scenes? If they can't, you are telling them the scenes. This is another area where a pair of objective eyes would prove priceless.

Another common encounter is the narrator telling the reader a character's real intentions or meaning.

Example

'I love you, Jim,' said Hannah. She meant it.

By this point, if it's not clear to the reader that Hannah really means it when she tells Jim she loves him, consider revising the whole previous part of the book in order to make it clear by *showing* it. Simply *telling* the reader 'She meant it' shows nothing but your narrator's lack of confidence in you and the reader.

If you feel the previous part of the story is just perfect the way it is and any alterations would only damage it, you could consider, *'I love you, Jim,' said Hannah and held his gaze for a few seconds longer. 'I really do.'* This revision shows us what the 'she meant it' told us. Common variations of the same instance, i.e. the narrator telling us what the characters really mean behind their dialogue lines is *he lied, she told the truth, he wondered, he hesitated* and so on.

Example

'I'm OK,' he lied.

There should be no need for this attribution; readers should know by now if he's lying or telling the truth.

Or,

Jim trusted the President, not knowing the President was no more than the puppet figure of an oppressive regime.

In the example above hopefully you have not only spotted the blunt telling, but the inconsistency in the point of view too. It is indeed a narrative slip, where the subjective narrator gains omniscient power in the author's eagerness to make sure we understand clearly what that President is truly about. I will come back to this example at the end of the book to illustrate the synergetic way of editing your own writing.

What can report writing do for your book? It can certainly move the story forward. Jim did A, Hannah answered B. But that's about it. It doesn't say how, why, when Jim did A and how, why, when Hannah answered. When you show, don't tell, your characterisation is the by-product of your narrative. It feels natural and unforced, organically and effortlessly taking shape with every paragraph. When you tell, your book is a mere collection of info-blocks put together and dumped onto the reader. Telling not showing is when your narrator doesn't trust you, the author, to do a good enough job so it steps in to help things along the way with the odd summarisation.

Showing, not telling means creating a word picture instead of a block description. It also means organic character development instead of block characterisation. It means building scenes with an enthralling atmosphere around them rather than telling us that Hannah felt this way and Jim did this followed by that. In other words, showing is fun, while telling is tedious and mind-numbing.

Exercise

Type in the Search box of your word processor 'sad'. Revise every instance and see if you can replace it with a more engaging description.

Summarisation

When you write, 'The following day, out of nowhere, Jim and Hannah decided to take a trip to the beach, spend some time in the local bars and do some shopping. They never expected to spend the whole week down there, it was such fun,' you *summarise* your own story for your readers. As with all examples in this book, this one is based on real writing.

After years of assessing fiction manuscripts, I can pretty much guarantee that a variation of the above example will show up in at least nine out of ten submissions at least once. And in seven out of the nine, it's likely to be towards the end of the book, where the author has run out of steam and the urge to finish takes over.

Summarisation is, without a shadow of a doubt, exceptionally bad writing. It reminds me of childhood story compositions, such as 'A Trip to the Zoo'.

> We arrived in the morning, we lined up, we fed the goat, we saw a crocodile, two giraffes, a baby elephant and his mummy. The highlight of the day was when we had an ice-cream, as it was a very hot day. Everybody arrived home tired, but excited to have spent an amazing day at the zoo. The end.

The only exciting thing about the above composition is the added 'as it was a very hot day' – it seems to give a little insight into the narrator's personality. So my point is, when you summarise, you don't allow for anything else, like style, atmosphere or character development.

Summarisation is not exposition. Exposition is your narrator letting us know what happens in the story by showing, not telling. Exposition adds continuously to your characterisation; while it can move the story forward at a great pace because it compacts the information in a block essay-style, summarisation skids past your characters at a hundred miles an hour, leaving your characters to pick up the pieces where they're dropped next time they are shown in action, not spoken about.

The good news is that it's easy to turn summarisation into scenes, and show your characters in action.

Example
I waited in the line, like everyone else. Once through the

gates, Lilly was the first one to grab a handful of grains and feed the goat straight from her hand. I didn't realise how tickly it felt until it was my turn.

This expository fragment gives us an insight into the character's thoughts and personality, thus adding to your characterisation. You really can turn *any* summarisation (no matter how silly!) into exposition and escape the telling trap.

The easiest way to detect summarisation in your manuscript is to stand in your readers' shoes and envisage how your reader would *summarise* a scene for someone else. Is it likely to be 'they arrived in the morning, they lined up, fed the goat, saw a crocodile, two giraffes, a baby elephant and his mummy. They had an ice-cream and everybody arrived home tired, but excited.' Do you have fragments like this in your manuscript? If yes, they are telling, not showing fragments and they should be turned into scenes one by one. You can then allow the reader to do the summarisation for you.

Showing and *telling*

Let's take this example:

Hannah was in a foul mood.

This is a particularly common variation of telling, not showing: showing *and* telling at the same time. You build a convincing scene, the right atmosphere, convincing dialogue, followed by telling us what the scene has just successfully showed.

Example

Hannah breathed deeply, her piercing eyes still pinning Jim to the wall. She kept her voice low and pressed on every word. 'Jim, I know we should try and make an effort for the sake of the kids, but right now I want to slash your stupid head off for being such a complete dickhead.' She paused for breath. 'You're wasting my time, Jim, get the hell out of my office!' she shrieked throwing her block of Post-its at him. Hannah was in a foul mood.

Why is showing, not telling important? Because it engages your reader by transporting them into the universe of your characters and thus it enhances the reading experience. Writing witness reports won't allow your readers to escape from their everyday lives into the extraordinary universe that is fiction and experience first-hand the amazing feelings and emotions your characters go through.

An unengaged audience is a lost audience and a major failure for the author and the editor. Readers kept at a distance and fed the message spoon by spoon will end up being alienated and will eventually give up on the book and very likely on the author's future books too.

The despairing truth is that telling is the most editing-resistant aspect of fiction writing. It comes across as stubborn and unwilling to shift when spotted. It requires extensive rewriting. If you ever doubt that your audience is capable of understanding artistic messages, join a readers' group or read readers' reviews of your favourite books.

Telling verbs, adverbs, phrases and figures of speech

As a tell-tale sign, instances in which you state how a character feels (for example, *he felt scared, he felt happy*, etc) are always telling, not showing. Also try to avoid adverbs such as *obviously, curiously, surprisingly* etc, as they are *telling* adverbs too. Phrases such as *to his great delight, against his wish, against all odds* etc are also signs of telling, not showing. The way to revise these is the same as with adverbs, use a stronger verb or a more descriptive action.

Example
Jim relaxed.

OK, this is as engaging as your latest car insurance policy. But consider,

> Jim lay back in the chair and crossed his ankles in front of him. He stretched his arms and closed his eyes, letting a deep sigh out.'

This innocent description is more vivid and atmospheric than 'Jim relaxed.'

Verbs that describe a state of being rather than an action are usually telling verbs.

> Hannah jumped. A plate was being placed onto the table with a bang, waking her up from her reverie.

as opposed to

Hannah jumped. The waiter slammed the plate onto the
table, waking her up from her reverie.

You will notice that in the first example, based on real writing, the
verb described the plate's state of being *and* that it required an extra
adverbial phrase, 'with a bang', as the author felt the verb wasn't
strong enough. In the edited version, the telling sentence was now
turned into a showing sentence: we have a dynamic picture in mind
of what happens in the scene. A plate is not just placed onto a table in
general – hard to imagine who or what placed it there – we have the
image of a waiter slamming the plate onto Hannah's table.

Passive verbs, verbs that describe a state of being – something is
happening to something else – are telling verbs. Aim to turn as many
passive verbs into active as you can during your self-editing process.
Avoid *-ing*-ending verbs and instead use concise and strong verbs that
don't require an adverb to make their message clear.

Remember, metaphors are showing, similes are telling. Notice the
difference between a metaphor and a simile conveying the same
message, the former showing, the latter telling as in this example:

'There was blood and tongues of fire above the blue-black
fjord and the city' (Edvard Munch, from a poem painted on
the frame of the 1895 pastel version of *The Scream*).

as opposed to

The sky was like blood and tongues of fire above the blue-
black fjord and the city.

Skies are not literally blood and fire tongues, but somehow we understand what Munch means, don't we? In the second example, we are told frankly that the sky was *like* blood and fire tongues, which somehow cancels the emotional impact the message has on us.

Metaphors need to still make sense though. Bad writing is cluttered with absurd metaphors gone wrong and sometimes I wish I had kept a collection of them as I encounter them not only in unpublished manuscripts, but in best-selling books too.

Example
The cars swam into the parking bay one after the other.

The cars swam? We guess the author intended to create a visual image of smooth driving into parking bays. But frankly cars can't swim, so the metaphor is wasted and silly. Sometimes your metaphors feel forced for the sake of overly wordy or artistic writing, but they are sure signs of bad writing.

Exercise

Open your manuscript and type in the Search box 'obviously'. Reread every instance in which you have used 'obviously' and decide whether it is telling, not showing. If it is telling, ditch it and rewrite the fragment, paying particular attention to scene and atmosphere this time. If you haven't started the editing yet, this is the ideal first step. Once finished with 'obviously', repeat the process with 'apparently', 'visibly', 'understandably', 'against his wish', 'he didn't want that to happen', 'he felt hopeless' etc.

Avoiding excessive adverbs and adjectives

My English teacher had a word for this, and he used it once while describing my attempts at prose-writing in Year 6. It was *Adjectivitis*. How is it that using a lot of adjectives and adverbs is always associated with bad writing? It even *sounds* like bad writing.

Example

'It was a dark and stormy night; the rain fell in torrents – except at occasional intervals, when it was checked by a violent gust of wind which swept up the streets (for it is in London that our scene lies), rattling along the housetops, and fiercely agitating the scanty flame of the lamps that struggled against the darkness.' (Edward George Bulwer-Lytton, *Paul Clifford*, 1830).

Five adjectives and an attributive clause at the end ('that struggled against the darkness') must be one of the major factors to make this fragment the tag line of the *Bulwer-Lytton Fiction Contest*. Checking the last few years' winning entries only confirms the statistics: the more adjectives and adverbs one uses, the worst the effect.

Excessively adding adverbs after your verbs is a firm sign of bad writing. It's a sign of weak verbs and the key to avoid this pitfall is to follow Strunk's and White's advice in *The Elements of Style*: use precise verbs to be concise. A precise verb is a verb strong enough to convey the intended message without the need to be modified by an adverb.

Example

He walked very fast back to his office.

as opposed to

He ran back to his office.

How can you replace an adverb without losing the message the adverb conveys?

'Ly' adverbs give fiction writing a heavy, overused feel. In the end, too many adverbs used too often will create a reading fatigue and your readers will develop a tendency of skipping them throughout the book.

The best technique of weeding out the overused adverbs is to combine the verb and adverb into a more suggestive verb.

Example
He walked confidently onto the stage, but failed miserably to cheer himself up.*

You can turn this into:

He marched on the stage,
he speeded up,
he hurried up,
he hastened,
he rushed,
he paced up, but could not cheer himself up.

---

*Apart from being a too common cliché, 'miserably' is a redundant add-on to the verb 'to fail', since all failures are supposed to be miserable after all.

So working your verbs harder is the easiest way to get a stronger, concise sentence.

Another technique would be to replace the verb-adverb with more descriptive action.

Example
He felt his confidence growing as he walked onto the stage, while still trying to cheer himself up.

To find all the adverbs ending in 'ly' in your manuscript, use the Find function on your word processor and type 'ly ' (don't ignore the necessary blank space at the end). Click Find and you will locate all the adverbs in the middle of your sentences. Consider revising them one by one. Type 'ly.' with the dot at the end and you will find all the adverbs at the end of your sentences. You can watch a short video on how to edit verbs in your fiction manuscript on my blog, www.self-editing.net

Being concise in your style doesn't mean being short or plain by any means. Your novel won't be checked against government standards for plain English. But at the same time overly wordy and stuffy English, or excessively old-fashioned narrative or long fragments written in unnatural language will not make anyone a great writer.

Stephen King compared adverbs in a manuscript to dandelions on a well-manicured lawn. One on its own looks pretty and cute. So when weeding your adverbs out of your manuscript, always remember that *Bulwer-Lytton* has a *-ly* in it.

One of the worst cases of bad writing is listing adjectives or adverbs.

Example

Hannah put on her favourite black, woollen, soft and cosy jumper.

Jim felt intrinsically, quintessentially and irrefutably sad.

The first sentence could be changed to *Hannah put on her cosy jumper*. The second, *Jim was sad*, which could be revised further to a description of Jim's sad state to avoid telling, not showing (see pages 51–63, *Telling, not Showing*).

If you have lists like these in your manuscript, cut them out right now. Pause reading and obliterate them. Unfortunately, writing like this sadly but irrefutably creeps through in some unedited self-published books, that's why if you decide to self-publish, you need to be a coldblooded self-editor.

> *Think of every adjective as a hundred-dollar bill and spend wisely.*
> (Raymond Obstfeld, *Novelist's Essential Guide to Crafting Scenes*)

Exercise

Following the method detailed in this chapter, open your manuscript and type 'ly ' (remember, without the quotation marks, but with the space at the end) in the Find box. You should have a number of all the -*ly*-ending adverbs in your manuscript that precede a space, not a punctuation mark. Just for the purpose of some practice, try to eliminate every fifth adverb by converting it into a more descriptive phrase or sentence. If you're happy with the result, keep it. If not, ditch it. When this is done, try finding 'ly.' or 'ly,' or 'ly?' and repeat the exercise. I bet you will replace at least ten dumb adverbs you haven't spotted while writing or revising your manuscript before and you will be pleased with your new result. Well done! You're one step further on the improvement scale.

Revising dialogue: Ockham's razor

Dialogue is what makes your story *sound* vivid and your characters *sound* real. Nothing seems to work quite as well in creating tension. But getting dialogue right is one of the trickiest tasks for any writer. Making characters sound real and *like themselves* is quite an intricate thing to craft.

When you revise the dialogue in your novel, a good starting point would be to trim it down.

A little theory now. William Ockham, the Middle Ages philosopher and logician, developed a principle that had a great career throughout the centuries, followed in almost all forms of humanities and sciences: 'Plurality must never be posited without necessity.'

In logic, this means that the hypothesis with the least assumptions should prevail.

In electronics, the simpler a system is, the more accurate its performance prediction is and the less chance of something going wrong with it.

In physics, it went as far as resulting in the hypothesis of the earth revolving around the Sun, being simpler to explain than the equally demonstrable hypothesis of other planets in the solar system revolving around the Earth, gaining the current general consensus.

In writing dialogue, it means keep it snappy. And don't quibble with me about the meaning of 'snappy'. No matter how sparse, chances are there is always too much dialogue in your manuscript because there is in most first-time manuscripts. Unless you're Jodi Picoult, hesitate to write page after page of nothing but dialogue.

Creative writing writer Nigel Watts said in his *Writing a Novel* guide, 'Dialogue is like a rose bush – it often improves after pruning.'

You can reduce dialogue in two ways:

1.   simply delete all redundant dialogue (see Example One below), or
2.   delete redundant dialogue and integrate the information it contained in the narrative (see Example Two on page 71).

In everyday speech, we use a lot of unnecessary words and we don't notice. We don't even notice long dialogues in movies. Because movies don't have a narrator like books do, they have to overcompensate through dialogue. So, in an attempt to make dialogue sound as natural as they can, many new writers write acres of needless dialogue that will either bore or exasperate any reader. Written words weigh heavier than spoken words. In a novel, readers will seek significance and scope in every word.

If you have any 'helloes' or 'goodbyes' or 'yes, of courses' in your dialogue, simply cut them out and replace them with characters' actions, reactions, thoughts, feelings, anything that might *show* the information contained in 'yes', 'no', 'hello', 'goodbye' etc.

Example One

'All done, I think we're ready to exchange signatures,' said the CEO.

'Yes, of course,' said Jim.

Here, 'Yes, of course' could be easily excluded and 'Jim smiled and signed' can replace it and still offer the same amount of information. Jim's smile shows he agrees with the CEO, a job 'Yes, of course' was meant to do.

I usually advise clients to cut out dialogue fragments like this every time I see them in manuscripts. Quite often though I receive back this kind of revision:

'All done, I think we're ready to exchange signatures,' said the CEO.

Jim didn't say anything and signed as indicated.

or

Jim just sat there, not saying anything, and signed.

This is very easy to revise. If a character doesn't say anything, just don't have it say anything in dialogue, without having the narrator tell the reader he or she doesn't say anything. This is basic showing, not telling. Just show the character doing (or not doing) the action.

An exception would be the necessity to show that the lack of dialogue is on purpose, such as in, *Hannah was speechless*. Use your own judgement and when dialogue or lack of dialogue is necessary, it needs to stay that way.

Example Two

Hannah arrived at the cafe´ a few minutes late.

'Hello,' she said and sat down at Jim's table.

'Hello,' said Jim.

'Sorry I'm late.'

'That's OK, don't worry about it.'

Instead of going through the helloes, consider replacing them with:

'Sorry I'm late,' said Hannah, sitting at Jim's table.

Because we have been told so many times *to write natural dialogue*, we try our best to write dialogue as we would naturally speak and act in a real-life conversation. However, the example above wastes readers' time and should not be seen in fiction. Again, once you become aware of this flaw, it becomes a joy to edit.

Another redundancy you should be hunting for is any unnecessary talk about the weather, about the time of the day, in fact any *unnecessary* talk at all.

But *unnecessary* is a fine distinction here. A long dialogue full of unnecessary talk could show a tension between the characters.

Example

Hannah arrived at the café a few minutes late.

'Hello,' she said and sat down at Jim's table.

'Hello,' said Jim.

'How are you?'

'Good, good, good. Yourself?' Jim kept the eye contact for a second longer.

'Yeah, good, thanks. Sorry I'm late,' she said and lowered her eyes.

'That's OK, don't worry about it.'

In the first example, dialogue is dull, long and unnecessary, in the second it is intriguing. So a safer way of looking at dialogue would be to cut out what doesn't contribute to the story or character development or atmosphere in any *relevant* way.

Exercise

Go through your novel with this filter of 'redundant dialogue' in mind and delete what can be easily deleted or deleted and reintegrated as narration as in the examples above.

Dialogue attribution

When you use anything other than *she said, he said* in your dialogue attribution, you risk bad writing. In the same way, adding more after *she said, he said*, such as adverbs and adverbial phrases, shows lack of confidence in your ability to write vivid and expressive dialogue.

Example
'You're not going to believe this,' Hannah said excitedly.

Instead of adding the dreadful and telling *excitedly*, you could consider changing the verb to incorporate the information 'Hannah said excitedly'. For instance, *'You're not going to believe this,' Hannah shouted.* Or perhaps *Hannah whispered.*

However, as you read through your dialogue, you will notice that the information about how characters talk is likely to be already conveyed in the larger context of your dialogue lines. In our case, it's very likely that only an excited person will say, 'You're not going to believe this,' shortly after we learn that Hannah has found the long-lost key to her 1979 Alfa Romeo.

One of my all-time favourite add-ons is 'simply' added to 'she said' or 'he said'. If he or she said it simply, this is the ultimate reason to *not* elaborate and keep it simple. She said, he said have a certain transparency about them, readers see these tags lines so much throughout a book, that they develop a blind eye to them, allowing focus to stay on what the characters actually say.

Good self-editing is weeding out all the unnecessary adverbs and you will see that, as you edit your manuscript, most of the information adverbs in tag lines convey is already conveyed in the context for the reader to realise how your characters say their dialogue lines at any given time. Be aware of long tag lines, they're almost always unnecessary and can misdirect focus from the dialogue line itself.

Do you need to add *she said, he said* after every single dialogue line? Most certainly not. In fact, if you feel you need to because it's not clear enough who's speaking, you need to go back over your dialogue and refine it until characters get their own clear voices. If it's a dialogue between two characters only, you will hardly ever have to add tag lines.

Asked or said?

'Where have you been?' Jim asked.

It's better to use *said* and not *asked*, after a question. The punctuation does the job for you here and shows the reader what *asked* tells them. There is a fine line here between *asked* and *demanded*. I would personally replace *demanded* with *said* if the context shows Jim in an overall demanding disposition. But if the question starts a new chapter for instance and we don't have much information about the larger context, *demanded* might just do a better job than *asked*, as it lets readers know pretty much straightaway that Jim is in a demanding mood. Again, use your judgement in the context of each paragraph.

Resisting the urge to explain: overwriting

In the thirteenth century, the theologist Thomas Aquinas put it simply: 'If a thing can be done adequately by means of one, it is superfluous to do it by means of several; for we observe that nature does not employ two instruments if one suffices.' This is the same principle of simplicity that Ockham's razor is based on.

Writing more than it is necessary in the hope that the *correct* message gets through to the reader is another particularly common weakness in new writing. Overwriting is always a sign of poor writing skills and it shows lack of confidence in the author's own ability to convey the message artistically as well as in the reader's capability of comprehending an artistic message.

When overwriting, when telling, not showing, when using adverbs excessively, the author does the job for the readers, not fully trusting the readers to do a good job on their own. It's a completely natural fear, the fear of not being understood, the make or break of any writer's self-confidence. But trust me, the more you rewrite – that is the more you place yourself in opposition to your writing, in an editor's position – the more aware you become of your overwriting and telling.

Example
'Thank you, everyone. I think we're all tired and it's getting late. Let's start again in the morning.' Hannah was feeling exhausted and decided to wrap up the meeting for the day.

This is unapologetically bad writing. Still, you would be surprised how common it is.

But overwriting can be subtler than the ridiculous example (as always, based on real writing) above. Remember unnecessary adverbs?

When you say,

> 'Let's wrap up the meeting,' Hannah said hastily,

adding *hastily* means you are explaining and explaining is overwriting.

Resist the urge to explain is a saying in creative writing as famous as *show, don't tell.*

One last example here to illustrate an important point: readers will understand the message from the context you create, without being told frankly what you mean.

> Hannah lifted her head, eyes still closed. When she started speaking her voice sounded broken and low, 'Thank you, everyone. Let's start again in the morning.'

Here, you won't even need Hannah to tell the reader she's tired, let alone the narrator, simply because we got it in the first place.

Every time you overwrite, you fail to give your readers credit. Every time you write something in inverted commas, such as 'she hoped she wouldn't be too "pushy" with this', you tell your reader black on white, 'You really wouldn't get that if it wasn't for my quote marks, would you?'

When is overwriting OK?

Almost never. However, I tend to be more tolerant in the case of a children's book. For instance, I have encountered this fragment in a historical novel for 11–14 year olds:

'I know you're not afraid to die!'

It was clear that Garwin held the Saxon in high regard.

Is the explanation necessary? For an 11 year old, maybe. For a 14 year old, maybe not. So, again, use your own judgement and write with the archetype of your audience in mind when gauging what's overwriting and what's not.

As a principle, if your audience is anywhere over 14, overwriting is nothing short of unacceptable.

Being aware of other common style flaws

Tautologies

+ He was analysing the situation further thinking it over and over.

+ He thought to himself, he wondered to himself; she squinted her eyes; she clapped her hands; he nodded his head; he shrugged his shoulders; underground mine; small baby.

Colloquialism

+ Hannah and Jim saw stars in each other's eyes, so to speak.

+ In the same way, Hannah knew better.

Clichés

+ Jim felt the task was exciting, although slightly daunting.

+ Hannah failed miserably at the task.

+ At the end of the day, it was Hannah's job.

+ To be honest, it's no one's fault.

+ To anyone's standards, this is a shithole.

+ Hannah proved her ability to think outside the box once more.

+ At this moment in time, Jim still had no clue about Hannah's intention.

+ He was clutching at straws.

+ He turned my life upside down.

+ All money went towards some much-needed school equipment.

+ This was a recipe for disaster.

Clichés will make your book boring to read and easy to forget. Don't use any of these atrocious clichés unless it's in dialogue and consistent with a dull and unimaginative character. If this character happens to be the point-of-view character, this will be the ultimate recipe for disaster for your book.

Figures of speech gone wrong

One of the most effective ways of showing not telling in fiction is by using figures of speech. However, they can sometimes be used in the wrong way and fail to achieve the intended effect.

Metaphors gone wrong

'Her younger brother's wavy blond hair peeped around the edge of the door and grinned mischievously at her.' This is obviously a fault of logic: hair could not possibly peep and grin.

Similes gone wrong

'They embraced each other as tightly as that two-flavor entwined string cheese' (Fragment from the 2011 winning submission for the Bulwer-Lytton fiction writing contest, by Mariann Simms, www.bulwer-lytton.com)

Epithets gone wrong

Using epithets can be a powerful tool in achieving your intended effect. For example, Joyce's choice of 'snotgreen' and 'scrotumtightening' when describing the sea, as opposed to Homer's epithet of 'deep-dark wine' in the first chapter of *Ulysses*? Joyce's choice is certainly not random. If Homer's epithet makes us think of richness, warmth and indulgence, Joyce's choice makes us think of coldness, infection, emotionlessness. This illustrates the immense power word choices have in fiction.

If you use epithets, make sure they evoke your intended message. I'll discuss word choices in-depth in Chapter 5.

4 *Perfecting characterisation*

Getting a character right in fiction is hard work. To match characters in literary fiction – hugely reflective, inhumanely complex, deeply idiosyncratic – characters in commercial fiction need to have complex problem-solving capabilities, extraordinary powers to overcome insurmountable obstacles, deal with the good, the bad and ugly, all in individual and appropriate ways, follow an impossible quest and resolve it, and all this while acting, sounding, and thinking like any ordinary human being.

Choosing the right names

It's not a good idea to give a character a seemingly relevant name if you're not going to follow it through. Remember, the reader is always one step ahead of you. If your character is called De Ville in a fantasy or horror story which involves the Devil as a main source of menace, your reader will suspect De Ville will have something to do with it. Showing him praying or carrying out an act of exorcism is confusing.

Avoiding block characterisation

Try to avoid block descriptions such as, *In the hallway stood a man wearing a baggy black suit and behind him stood a woman with extremely feminine features,* as the reader is likely to forget instantly the details of your descriptions. Instead, consider adding one description detail at a time, as you go.

You could develop your characterisation by dotting the descriptive details along the way, in the shape:

(...) he said taking his baggy jacket off

or

Jim couldn't help but notice how soft the woman's face looked when she broke into a smile.

The same example also illustrates how important it is to give your characters memorable details when you introduce them. Something to stick in the reader's mind and help them associate a particular vision with a particular character. Would it be suitable for the man in the baggy suit to wear a Rolling Stones t-shirt underneath, the pink diamond tongue sticking out through the generously cut sides of his jacket? Would it be suitable for him to have a ponytail? Would it suit the woman to have arrived on the latest model Ducati?

Block descriptions are closely related to telling, not showing. What summarisation does for your style (see Summarisation on page 57), block characterisation does for your characterisation. All the style handicaps of summarisation are also valid for descriptions in block. If telling, not showing denies your readers experiencing first-hand, then block characterisation stops your readers from connecting with your characters on an emotional level.

Example

The truth is that Jim was a really nice guy, who doted on his children, even though at times they could tease him mercilessly, but he would always laugh it off and be in a good mood.

If there are fragments like this in your manuscript, consider turning them into scenes one by one and allowing your reader to summarise the *scene* for themselves and draw their own conclusions.

A safe principle of avoiding telling, not showing is to stay away from *abstractions*, such as generic names for emotions, attitudes, moods and so on. So instead of saying 'Jim was in a bad mood', create a scene and show him losing it. The same principle applies in characterisation. Is Jim a sad lad, in general? Resist the urge to state it. Is Hannah a happy soul? Don't say it. Is Adam an arrogant lothario? Resist it.

Allow your readers to learn about your characters by showing what they do, not by stating frankly what they're like. Show other characters' reaction to their beauty, don't state *Hannah was a beautiful tall blonde, with piercing blue eyes and a bright smile.* Don't say, *Jim had an effeminate manner,* show his flimsy wrists and elegant walk. Characterisation through plain stating has the same emotional effect on the reader as a roadside lamppost.

Block characterisation seems to stand out particularly in first-person narrators. We all know the old trick of using a mirror to describe a character's physical appearance. For example, avoid writing anything along the lines of: *Putting my hat on, I take one last look in the mirror before stepping out the door. Yes, a typical 30-year-old brunette, green eyes, luscious lips, high-arched cheeks, curls bouncing on the shoulders, pretty smile.*

Don't do this. If there is even a mention of a mirror episode in your manuscript, it's a sign that it needs a good looking at. How can you have a first-person character described if not by him- or herself? One easy technique you could try is to have the first-person character described by other characters in dialogue.

Example

This hat would go well with your dark curls.

Even so, other characters can still commit block characterisation for each other, so keep an eye out for it when revising.

Example

'This is not like Jim at all,' said Hannah. 'He never showed an interest in my business trips before, but last night he went all crazy. I mean he's far from stupid, but come on. I need some space here.'

Or

'Man, she's gorgeous. Just look at her. Dark hair, dark but bright eyes, beautiful lips, perfectly white teeth, a badass personality...she's just my type!'

An extreme variation is when the protagonist shows unashamed self-adoration.

Example

Jim lifted his hand to eye level and watched it intently while it was turning as if in slow motion. 'The hand of a pianist indeed!' he sighed.

This type of characterisation is particularly embarrassing when minor characters show adoration for the hero too, stating frankly how intelligent he or she is and how amazing it is that they could overcome a particular obstacle.

Example

'Only Jim could have figured this out,' said Hannah. 'It's his sheer intelligence, the way he planned it all and the way he deciphered the code – I mean no one else could have come up with an idea like this.'

You guessed it, this is disguised self-adoration from the author here. It's the author in the first place who designed the whole plot and by having his or her characters praise each other's intelligence or genius and the brilliance of the whole plan, we can almost see the author blushing and nodding his or her head discreetly in acceptance of the compliment. It's safe to stay away from this type of discounted self-gratification as it rarely achieves the intended effect on the reader. It really is easy not to have characters state each other's brilliance and trust the readers to appreciate the brilliance of a situation or solution in the story. Resist stating it.

When trying to avoid block characterisations, some writers go too far in their attempt to suggest what the character is like. For example, saying 'She had the shivering nostrils of a noble mare' about a pretty ballerina is really a description that does not fit the purpose in any way.

Exercises

1. To decide if your characterisation is based on telling, not showing, take the first-person character test. Would your characters say, 'I have brown hair, I wear a blue coat and I have black eyes'? No. So don't have your third-person character say it either.

2. Get a project book, the type with sections in it. Name your sections after your main characters, one by one.

Start reading your whole manuscript with only *block characterisation* in mind. Your protagonist would be a good start. Revise nothing else, but telling, not showing and block information about each character. As you read, copy in handwriting on your notebook all the blocks of characterisation you find in your manuscript, in their respective sections.
When you have finished reading and copying, it's time to start revising. Add, cut, rewrite and revise, see where else in the manuscript you could fit bits of information from the blocks. As you finish with one fragment, cross it out in your notebook or tear the page off and discard it.

Recognising unempathic characters

Lack of empathy towards your characters from your readers is another serious failure that leads to an unengaged audience. Does your audience *care* enough about your characters to follow their story until the end? Do they care if your protagonist gets trapped in a seemingly inescapable situation? Do they feel anger when he or she gets bullied, tortured, lied to, cheated on? Are they satisfied when he or she overcomes obstacle after obstacle? If your protagonist encounters so much as being talked down to in the corner shop and the readers don't feel outraged by it, he or she is a failed protagonist. If your villain as much as gets away with lying to a character who appears in the story two or three times and the readers don't feel mad at the conniving shit, he or she is a failed villain and a weak villain is no match for a great protagonist.

Avoiding dull characters: John Smith and Jane Roe

It's an appealing idea to create a completely ordinary character and perhaps even call him John Smith or Jane Roe. This kind of protagonist is the most popular in fiction for the very reason that most of us can identify with him or her and relate to their type of issues. However, at some point in the story, not too late, we will expect John or Jane to do or at least think or feel or say something out of the ordinary that would make us want to know more about them. Something that would keep us intrigued about their story's ending.

Unfortunately, many first-time writers asking us to assess their manuscripts get stuck around this point, when it comes to giving their characters an edge.

Characters who are so squeaky clean, conservative and monotonous they could feature in any Disney production are frankly boring. To stay away from dull and uninteresting protagonists, give them a special feature, *an edge*. Why? Because an edge makes characters mesmerising and hard to forget. Trap them in a set of extraordinary circumstances so we can see how they react. Have them react to extreme pressure and show their edgy side.

An internal conflict is a popular choice with writers who receive this suggestion. However, very rarely is an internal conflict strong enough to make the character jump off the page with liveliness.

Example

Anastasia Steele is a completely normal 22-year-old college student. There's not much extraordinary about her — her looks or her personality. In fact nothing at all, except that she is a virgin who accepts to sign a dominance/submission contract with an attractive and disconcerting Christian Grey and later asks him to beat her up with a belt. Who would do that, right?

Intriguing? Yes, as far as Anastasia Steele is concerned, her character has just gained a new dimension. 'There is more to this girl than meets the eye,' I hear the reader say, 'let's see what else she's capable of.'

There is nothing in fiction more captivating than an unusual POV character. As readers, the temptation of experiencing a completely new and unusual perspective over everything is hard to resist. Personally, I'm extremely fond of Christopher Boone, the narrator in Mark Haddon's *The Curious Incident of the Dog in the Night Time* and of Jack, the five-year-old narrator in Emma Donoghue's *Room*. They both have a strong edge to them, their conditions, which makes them both mesmerising and addictive.

You don't need to go to these extreme lengths to give your characters and especially your narrators an edge, but it's a wasted chance to let them sink in complete dullness, together with your book.

Discarding 'Random Jim' characters

Over the years of working with new writing, I have noticed that the likeliness of unempathic characters increases with the number of characters in the story. The more characters you introduce in your story, the more likely it is that they will be underdeveloped, unempathic and perhaps even easy to forget along the way. It's good practice to keep the number of characters to those who are *necessary*. As a principle, never use a random character to solve a new situation.

Example

As Hannah was struggling with the latest spreadsheet, she spotted a newcomer passing her office.

'Excuse me,' she shouted. 'You're Jim from Accounts, right?'

'Yes...' said the newcomer with that perplexed newcomer look on his face.

This is OK at the beginning of the book, but definitely not OK on page 85 out of 120, when the story has a sufficient cast to move it forward and the readers know everything about everyone in the story. However, I have encountered many authors who create a seemingly inescapable situation for their protagonist and thus achieve the impressing effect on the reader, only to introduce a new character out of nowhere who solves the problem. No, we didn't predict this, but this is nonetheless bad and annoying writing. In literary theory, this is largely called *deus ex machina* (see page 17). The term comes from Ancient Greek plays where a God would be lowered onto the stage by a pulley and resolve the situation. Hence the name, 'God from the machine'.

Deus ex machina is not restricted only to new or random characters happening to be passing by just when they're needed. It can refer to new-found objects, undiscovered abilities, like a black belt the protagonist forgot he had only to come back when he is mobbed by a local gang and so on.

The way to avoid *deus ex machina* is to employ more of the *Chekhov's Rifle* technique. Is your protagonist a black belt? Make sure you mention this detail about him or her before the detail is needed to resolve an unexpected situation.

As a principle, it should be the characters who create circumstances and not the other way around.

But, I hear you saying, how does one introduce new characters without using new circumstances?

One way to avoid the 'random Jim' flaw would be to introduce all characters at the beginning of the story and use *Chekhov's Rifle* to pull them out of the hat when a new situation that requires them arises.

Example

Jim is introduced on page 4 in dialogue with Hannah, only to be used on page 85 when his expertise is needed.

The same can be said about a *new* best friend, who appears out of nowhere in the middle or towards the end of the book, with the single purpose to offer a shoulder to cry on to the protagonist, so the readers (a) get a deeper characterisation of the protagonist, and (b) find out more about the story behind the events. Surely, by now, a best friend is something we should already know about.

Being aware of stereotypical 'Australian Sheila' characters

A compelling character is a believable and life-like character by all accounts. A professor of English speaking like Busta Rhymes at the Royal Wedding would be a pretty unconvincing occurrence in fiction. In real life, it can happen and it would be classed as extraordinary and original. In fiction it would be seen as plain silly.

What is a stereotypical character? An Australian carrying a kangaroo in Amsterdam behind a Japanese tourist taking a photograph. Come on. Real life could easily allow for this instance to take place, but fiction simply needs to be more reasonable than life itself.

Stereotypical characters are annoying and often offensive. They seem to be everyone's favourite pick-on at readers' groups meetings. Readers love to destroy an author who uses a drunken Irishman in his or her book. I am particularly fond of good-looking, hardworking but poor Eastern Europeans, working illegally and always getting lost in London. Female readers seem to be particularly slighted by objectified women, like the long-legged secretary wearing a pencil skirt always 'hugging her hips', the unattractive and often overweight, but highly successful female lawyer or CEO and so on.

A stereotypical character is the height of one-dimensional characters. These characters are often called *stock characters* because they only seem to possess attributes that fit their role in the story. Characters like these could never build empathy with the readers, they could never be taken seriously. In fact classic authors used stereotypes as caricature in social satires and comedy. These characters were called *tippi fissi* (fixed types) in Commedia dell'Arte in Italian literature, and types such the avarist, the misogynist, the adulterer, the naïve, the cunning one and so on have a long literary career starting with Ancient Greek comedy.

From a writer's perspective, anyone can appreciate the appeal of stock characters. They're ready-made, easy to stick onto any scene. They don't require building up, anyone will 'get' them; after all, we've all encountered them before. From a reader's perspective though, stock characters are awful and unbearable.

Developing 'Rigid Jim' characters

Sometimes called *character development* in literary criticism, major characters in fiction often undergo a transformation caused or fuelled by the events they're going through.

Good character development is achieved gradually, where changes follow significant events in the story. For example, we understand why, after seeing her ex with a new girlfriend, who happens to be beautiful, Hannah feels the urge to start a diet the very same day and she joins a dating site. She never mentioned it before, but it just makes sense and no further explanations are required.

In the same way you build a strong plot based on the action–consequences structure (see Chapter 1), you build a strong, compelling and consistent character based on the same action–consequences structure. A character needs to make sense, his or her actions and reactions need to make sense to avoid that dreadful randomness and inconsistency so often encountered in first-time writing characters.

If you show potential for change at the beginning of the book, you not only open up the opportunity for character development, but you have already added a deeper dimension to your character. The way to do it is to learn from literary fiction titles, where a character is never the same at the beginning and the end of the story.

A popular choice in commercial fiction is to show how a character grows stronger because of the obstacles he or she encounters, which show one of their biggest weaknesses that he or she will overcome. Readers will associate this with the character's inner transformation.

Example

Hannah's biggest fear is to drive over High Mountain Bridge. The story opens with her sweating in the car, which is jamming the traffic at the entrance on the bridge. She cannot force herself to move forward, despite the long queue of cars forming behind her and the blaring horns.

The dénouement sees Hannah hesitating to go over the bridge, but pressing the accelerator and driving over High Mountain Bridge while feeling like she has just achieved the greatest thing ever.

My favourite characters are this type of character; those who start out and end like any of us, but have the power to inspire us to overcome the obstacles in our own lives we would usually think of as insurmountable. My all-time favourite ending is in *The Curious*

Incident in the Night-time. It's a powerful and inspiring scene, as Christopher Boone, a 15 year old with Asperger's syndrome, after realising he has travelled to London on his own and succeeded in finding his estranged mother, says, 'I can do anything.' How powerful is that? Imagining his euphoria at the realisation that *he can do anything* still gives me goosebumps.

Do you believe in the power fictional characters have over real people? The way they influence our lives and ultimately change it?

In an informal survey conducted by HuffPost Books on Facebook, some of the most influential characters were Atticus Finch, Pi Patel and Jay Gatsby. Some people confessed they have named their kids after fictional characters (Holden was a popular choice), others confessed they learnt stoicism, perseverance, courage, sensitivity and empathy from books. One reader said, 'Oh my, almost everyone I read. I am partially composed of all the book characters I've read over the years.' Ultimately, we are all living our lives under continuous cultural conditioning.

For me, reading Albert Camus when I was 15 changed me in a radical way. Nothing else would have had the same effect in the way I saw the world from then on. Around the same time, I was reading a lot of contemporary Romanian writers (since this was the country I was born and brought up in), including Simona Popescu, a very young novelist at the time. Her coming-of-age novel, *Exuviae*, had a similar effect on my formation. In a way, it educated my femininity and taught me to think and see the world like a girl, with everything that's involved – sensitivity, passion, authenticity, closeness – as well as self-interest to the point of absolute self-centredness.

After my teen years, there were a lot of other influential characters I encountered, but none of them had the impact the existentialist ones had on me.

And this is my point: we, as human beings, and the way we live our lives, are constantly modelled by the culture we live in and literature, perhaps more than anything else, plays a hugely important role in all of it. We learn to suffer from Anna Karenina and Juliet Capulet. We learn stoicism from Pi Patel and principles from Atticus Finch. We learn introspection and find appeal in self-doubt from Holden Caulfield.

What is literature ultimately about? I believe we love literature because it allows us to learn how other people live their lives and because it makes us feel good. Books make us feel extraordinary and help us escape our own insipid lives.

Give your characters flaws, make them human and worthy of our following their story. Show them overcoming extraordinary obstacles and believe in the power they can have over real people's lives.

Dealing with inconsistent characterisation

It's frustrating not to make sense of a character in a book. It's fun when we keep getting bits about them, bits that we can put together and build the bigger picture. But sometimes the bits are so contradictory, it's hard to understand what a character is about. Conflicting aspects about a character are like misshaped pieces in a jigsaw: no matter how hard you try to fit them together, you will only emphasise their misfit.

How to fix an inconsistent characterisation

Some authors find that making a clear statement about each character helps them focus their angle more accurately on what needs to stay and what needs to go in the build of that particular character. This is an immensely powerful tool, very easy to use and very efficient. Sometimes the statement could be the summarisation your readers will make about your character at their readers' group meeting or how Wikipedia might describe your character. The quiz in the exercise at the end of this chapter will help you plan your characters and their actions better.

Example

'Mr Bennet is a bookish and intelligent gentleman with a wife and five daughters. He is amused by the indecorous manners and nonsense of his wife and three younger daughters, and he offers little beyond mockery by way of correcting them. He relates very well with his two eldest daughters, particularly Elizabeth, showing them much more respect than his wife and younger daughters.' (From the Wikipedia article on Jane Austen's *Pride and Prejudice*.)

This is the type of statement that Jane Austen could have written in her notebook to help her keep Mr Bennet's characterisation consistent and flowing.

While we were preparing Joanna Price's *A Means of Escape* for print, we were shocked to receive a back-page blurb from a copywriter referring to Rob Brown, a main character we perceived to be quite charming, witty and, OK, maybe a little overconfident too, as a 'chauvinistic superior'. The author emailed me her reaction and added that, yes, Brown might be arrogant, but deep down he respects women and cares about them. I strongly think that the very fact that Joanna wrote this particular statement about Rob Brown in an email to me, helped her focus her characterisation with higher care in the second book in the series, where no mention of chauvinism was made by anyone, albeit Brown is still just as arrogant.

'Personality sheets' or sections in a project notebook, as suggested in the avoiding block characterisation section on page 81, will help tremendously. If you're the planning type, you have probably already written them while you were planning your novel. If you haven't done them yet, it's time to write one for each character. 'What is the point of personality sheets? I am the God of my Universe, the maker of my characters, I can create them as I go, in any way I want, so what is the point?' I hear some of you asking. The answer is simple: if you go with the flow and create your characters perhaps not entirely randomly, but not tight enough either, chances are you will create inconsistent or even clashing personalities for your characters.

As a literary consultant, picking on character inconsistencies has to be my favourite activity of all. I love personality sheets and I make handwritten ones on larger Post-Its for every major character in a novel or short story I assess. If a character has the wrong colour underwear, I love to pick on it and point it out in my report. For example, why would Dr Ballantine choose to drink vodka at the reception? He lived in Aberdeen all his life, so if there's a strong reason for him not to choose whisky at the reception, only then does vodka become an understandable choice. However, I know that readers would like to see Dr Ballantine drink vodka because that adds to his freshness and works against him as a stereotype character. So have him choose vodka if the type of characterisation you have built for him so far was unconventional in every other way.

As you can see, the line between building a consistent character and a stereotype is a very fine one that needs handling with a lot of care.

Exercise

Write a main statement about your protagonist and keep it on your desk, at hand every time you read through your manuscript, as you carry out the revision. Once it's at the forefront of your mind, you will soon start to find instances that don't quite fit the character. Doing the quiz at the end of the chapter will help too.

Repeat the exercise with the rest of the characters.

Adding complexity to underdeveloped characters

A particularly common weakness of first-time novels is an *underdeveloped villain*. Most of the time, the villain is a two-dimensional character, in the story for one single reason – to create some menace for the protagonist – and in his or her quest to do just that he or she forgets to do anything else.

Take this example:

> Jim drew his face closer to Hannah's face, so, when he started to speak, a spray of spit landed on Hannah's face.
>
> 'You park in my spot once more, make sure you check your tyres.'

The dialogue could continue for pages and pages, where Jim tries to intimidate Hannah. What is wrong with this? Well, first of all, this kind of menace could well be found in a children's novel. Victor Hazell tries to intimidate little Danny and his father in Roald Dahl's *Danny, the Champion of the World* by coming across as simply nasty in the way he talks to them. Yes, this adds to the reality of your character, but the menace a villain poses needs to build up so convincingly, it can well be that it gives readers the chills – which is an experience readers seek.

An underdeveloped character is often referred to as a 'stock' or 'cardboard' character, a 'two-dimensional' character. In essence it is a character lacking complexity, with a single purpose, usually to move the story forward in some way. How can you turn a cardboard character into a compelling character? One way of doing this would be by adding complexity. A character who is a mixture of good and bad is a character with the potential to change. His or her metamorphosis can add depth to his or her portrayal and engage the reader onto more than the story level.

Toning down overdeveloped characters

Sometimes characters can be overdeveloped with terrible effects. Giving a minor character an *over-described* past or an *irrelevant* past would be a good example. Sometimes we just don't need the amount of characterisation we are given to understand or empathise with a character.

Example

Sophie was keen to end the conversation as she was due to meet a lawyer she had met through a dating agency for a second date in a wine bar in the town centre and did not want to be late. They had seemed to click on the first date and this was the only one the agency had recommended who had seemed to be any good, or at least half normal.

We really don't need to know this about Sophie, she is a minor character who never appears again in the story. If you want to make us understand why she is in a hurry when she has this conversation – because her being in a hurry is necessary to the later development of the plot – consider introducing her earlier, showing her meeting up with the lawyer from the agency and resolving to go on a second date on the day of the conversation or at least show her mentioning this to someone. When you then mention she is in a hurry, we remember why and your writing delivers an already improved reading experience.

Informing readers about unknown villains

If you have a minor villain in your story, such as a traitor, make sure we know about them before they turn out to be a villain. There is no pleasure in discovering a suspect, if we don't *suspect* him/her in the first place. In a fantasy thriller, one of our clients had us read the first five first chapters in which we were anticipating discovering who the traitor in a spoiled plan was. In chapter six, it was a completely unknown police officer we hadn't read about in the first five chapters, who has never been mentioned in dialogue or narrative, a completely new character to be given such an important role. Needless to say that the character came across as crassly undeveloped and less than two-dimensional because it was there to serve only one purpose in one single context, and it made an otherwise entertaining story feel random and extremely weak.

Limiting the number of named characters

A quick fix for this issue would be to keep the number of named characters to important characters only. A detective passing briefly by the scene of the crime with no importance at all in the later development of the story doesn't need to appear as 'Detective Constable Jim Parker', can be easily replaced with 'a detective'. Name dropping is a sure way to add to readers' tiredness.

The 'Random Jim' trick *never* works so it should be added on your to-be-edited list without delay.

Exercise

Make a list of all the major characters in your story starting with the protagonist and continuing with the antagonist. For each one of them, complete the following quiz:

What do I look like?

What do I wear right now?

What would I wear on a first date?

What music do I listen to? Write down my iTunes Faves playlist.

How do I take my coffee?

Do I like sleeping alone?

What have I had for breakfast today?

Have I ever been late for a meeting?

Would I ever be rude to someone?

What is my dark side?

What is my edgiest trait?

5 Crafting memorable scenes and atmosphere

If your readers are to remember any of your characters, they will always remember them *within a scene* – doing something within it, or just being part of it. As readers, we are more likely to remember scenes than dialogue lines. And if there ever were a thing desperately aiming to be memorable, that would be a dialogue line.

Closely related to *telling, not showing*, not crafting an inspiring or memorable scene, with an appropriate atmosphere, is a particularly common oversight in new writing.

Example

'Leaning over the sink, she looked in the mirror and resolved to leave Jim.'

A paragraph later, Hannah is alone in bed recounting the break-up with Jim. We get the ultimate telling, not showing mantra, 'She felt lonely', soon after.

In both cases, the hypothetical author misses a great opportunity to build a truly memorable scene. Instead of simply saying, 'she resolved to leave Jim', use anything in your power to *make us understand* her resolution. And most of the time, constructing a scene is the best tool in the box.

You could use an object, say a diamond pendant Jim gave her for her birthday (the object should have been already mentioned earlier in the story, see *Chekhov's Rifle* on pages 15 and 22). You could make her take the pendant off and stare at it for a second. Through blurry eyes perhaps, if this fits your style. Make her look back in the mirror and then back at the pendant, thus suggesting a contrast between herself and her relationship with Jim and her hesitation. Does she really want him? What has she become since they've been together? What would she be like without him? Make her drop the pendant and wash it down the drain. You see how from a simple 'she resolved to leave Jim', you could develop an evocative scene that could haunt us for a long time.

The more sophisticated your audience is, the more sophisticated your writing needs to be, i.e. the more surprising and memorable your scenes need to be. Using generic scenes, like starring blankly out of a window to describe sadness, won't cut it with your readers. Remember Strunk and White's principle mentioned earlier: 'Prefer the specific to the general, the definite to the vague, the concrete to the abstract.' (*Elements of Style*)

How to recognise a poor scene

How does a scene fail? A scene fails when it misdirects the reader's focus away from the story through a combination of poor word choices, lack of dramatic effects, lack of atmosphere and bad setting.

Every scene in your book should have a *purpose* and a *focus*. Scenes that don't have either are random scenes and they can be safely excluded without any effect on the story at all.

The *purpose* of a scene is the goal it achieves in the story. For instance, a scene in which Jim is shown in the gym, training in karate, has the purpose of telling us that Jim has a certain skill he is likely to need later on in the story.

The *focus* of this scene is to make the readers know this detail about Jim, so they understand why he defeats his opponents a few chapters later when he is attacked.

This purpose–focus test proves this to be a good scene, i.e. a scene that needs to be kept, as it achieves both. You now know how to test every scene in your novel or short story and edit those that don't achieve one or both, by either deleting them, or giving them a purpose when they don't have one and focusing them better so they achieve the intended effect on the reader. The exercise at the end of this chapter will help you further.

Another particularly persistent flaw in new writing is the dreaded *information dump*. The author is so eager to earn his or her readers' credibility, that he or she stops the story dead in its tracks with a big block of research information. An information dump on technology, how a certain gadget works, measurements, etc., can kill a scene instantly, so don't do it. And if you have done it, delete it immediately.

Making appropriate word choices

In her excellent book, *Reading like a Writer*, Francine Prose says,

'The ability to look at a sentence and see what's superfluous, what can be altered, revised, expanded, or especially cut, is essential.' This could easily be the mantra of any conscious self-editor writer.

Like the style and the narrative, the choice of words runs vertically through your book, touching every one of its levels. Yet, it seems it becomes crucial when crafting *scenes*. The words you choose can make or break a scene, because scenes depend so much on atmosphere and on what they are meant to evoke for the reader.

Example

'A musky tang of oil and steam drifted in wreaths through Rice Lane from the cargo ships at West India Dock, mingling with the soot and smoke of a thousand coal fires. The factories at Wapping beat a steady throb while their chimneys pointed to a sapphire sky.' (Original unedited opening paragraph of Allan Watts' *Touched by Angels*)

In my opinion, this is a beautiful opening. I absolutely loved the word 'sapphire' in the context. So much so, that it made it very tough for me to change it to 'slate' in the finished version of the book. Why? Well, 'sapphire' doesn't say much about the sky. Skies usually come in blue, albeit variant shades of it. Slate is also arguably a shade of blue, after all, I've encountered the phrase *slate-blue* before and the *Oxford Dictionary of English* defines 'slate-coloured' as 'of a dark bluish or greenish grey'. So why did I change the beautiful choice of opulent and attractive 'sapphire' with the oppressive, harsh and heavy 'slate'? *Touched by Angels* is the story of an oppressed woman and her nine-year-old son living in abysmal poverty in industrial London at the beginning of the 20th century, a woman who goes to extreme lengths to escape her situation. 'Slate', even though it might not sound as well in the rhythm of the paragraph, adds more to the atmosphere of the scene and evokes the oppression and despair of those people; so these are the two main reasons for my choice. Luckily, the author liked it and this is how it appears in the published edition.

This is a particularly good example of why self-editing is so necessary. When you reread your scenes, you have the time to stop and think if the words you chose are the best choice in the context of your scene, if they add to the scene, rather than detract from it or its feel. Once you work with this filter in mind, you will be able to revise and rewrite your scenes in order to achieve a more persuasive effect.

Setting the tone of a scene

Word choices set *the tone* of a scene too. The same scene can be defined as *warm*, *cold*, *distant* or *engaging* depending on the choice of words used.

Example

The lamp lit up with a soft tick. The room sank in a golden glow and the 9mm Beretta glinted briefly before pointing at me.

Words like *soft*, *tick*, *golden*, *glow*, *glinted* make the scene feel warm and almost cosy, which is unexpected in the context of a gun pointing at the POV character. This choice of words would suit a particular scene if you want *to show* the character is relaxed and confident because, despite the gun pointing at him or her, they have things under control. Simply by using warm words you show a scene's tone and save yourself from having to add, 'But I've got things under control.' By reading the character's description of the room, we should get a feeling about the way the character approaches the situation, without having to be *told* so.

Compare this to:

> The lamp lit up with a snap. The room was illuminated and the 9mm Beretta flashed quickly before pointing at me.

Words such as *snap*, *illuminated*, *flashed* inspire coldness and even fear at having been surprised (*snap*), discovered (*illuminated*) and exposed (*flashed*). We instantly know the character doesn't feel as safe and confident about being confronted with a gun.

My message here is the same: you don't have to tell the message to the reader. You only have to suggest it.

In the same way, avoid using extreme-power words that would choke any scene or swamp it in excessive melodrama.

Example
> Pain rises up in my chest and my heart explodes under such excruciating pressure.

You can almost hear the reader coughing gently in embarrassment.

Using word choices to direct narrative

Let's take this example:

> 'The forehead was high and very pale, and singularly placid; and the once jetty hair fell partially over it and overshadowed

> the hollowed temples with innumerable ringlets, now of a
> vivid yellow, and jarring discordantly in their fantastic
> character with the reigning melancholy of the countenance.'
> (E. A. Poe, *Berenice*)

Notice how Poe used suggestive adjectives (*pale, placid, jetty, hollowed, vivid*) to create a high contrast, without simply stating Berenice was ill. What does this fragment tell us about the *narrator* though? The narrator here is first-person Egaeus, gradually becoming obsessed with Berenice's decline. The level of detail he goes to in order to describe Berenice's illness is representative for how obsessed he becomes with it. The words your point-of-view character chooses to paint a picture in the reader's mind must be consistent with that particular character's thoughts and feelings. I have insisted in *Determining the point of view* (page 26) that, if you have a subjective narrator, i.e. the story is narrated through the POV of a particular character, that point of view could not possibly be neutral. This is also valid for describing scenes, setting and choosing the right words a particular character would choose in keeping with his or her characterisation. By keeping everything consistent, you ensure you have a convincing and enthralling narrative as well as a consistent characterisation.

It's this kind of detail that sets atmosphere and angle around every one of your scenes and, the more you work on your choice of words, the more finesse and quality you will give to your writing.

Using unnecessary words

A piece of favourite advice given by most writing experts is to omit needless words. Strunk and White in *Elements of Style*, couldn't be clearer on this:

*'Vigorous writing is concise. A sentence should contain no
unnecessary words, a paragraph no unnecessary sentences,
for the same reason that a drawing should have no
unnecessary lines and a machine no unnecessary parts. This
requires not that the writer make all his sentences short, or
that he avoid all detail and treat his subjects only in
outline, but that every word tell.'*

Strunk and White's examples include changing 'the question as to
whether' to 'whether', 'this is a subject which' to 'this subject', 'his
brother, who is a member of the same firm' to 'his brother, a member
of the same firm', thus eliminating superfluous words 'who is', and
'owing to the fact that' to 'since' or 'in spite of the fact that' to
'though', thus eliminating the 'debilitating expression', *the fact that.*

To these, I could add a new category of pleonastic constructions,
such as, *She nodded her head, He clapped his hands, She squinted
her eyes, He shrugged his shoulders, She blinked her eyes, He sat down
on the couch, She sent out the mail to editors.*

Overcoming a lack of dramatic effect

Scenes in fiction work particularly well in giving characters depth,
building a memorable setting, cooling down action episodes or
adding dramatic effect where it's really needed.

Example

Jim took the weapon and handed it to a guard. Then he
forced Hannah and Adam to stand facing each other. Then he
pulled a knife out of his pocket and stabbed Hannah in the
heart. The blood streamed down her white dress all over the
marble floor. Her friend was flustered by this happening.

> With her last strength, Hannah hugged Adam and they
> immediately felt an immediate love that words cannot explain.
> But it was too late.

You see, being a literary consultant is not always fun and games. Sometimes you can be at a complete loss about your job, as when you receive something like the fragment above. You simply feel a despair that words cannot explain.

What is wrong with this fictional example based closely on the final paragraph of a fantasy novel we received for copy-editing? A lot of things, you might say, however, something seems to stand out particularly well. What's clearly meant to be a powerful scene is as immersive as a millpond to a triathlon-approved lifebuoy. Unfortunately, the dramatic action taking place doesn't compensate for the absolute lack of emotion and drama. In fact, so much so, that it stops what could be a tremendously powerful scene from being a scene at all. Again, it's a pointless witness report.

Example One

> Jim pulled a knife out and stabbed Hannah in the heart.

Compare to:

> Jim pulled the knife out and top and tailed the gooseberries
> for tonight's party.

Example Two

> The blood streamed down her white dress all over the
> marble floor.

Compare to:

The strawberry juice sprayed all over Hannah's white dress.

Even the strawberry juice accident would get a more dramatic reaction from Hannah and from the reader than the matter-of-fact stabbing in our example.

As much as they lack realism, some of your scenes will lack proportionate drama and estimating the right amount of drama in every scene can be a tricky task. The following exercise will aim to act as an estimate gauge.

Exercise

Locate the scene that you intend to be the most dramatic in your book. The climax would qualify as a good candidate. Start rereading it looking for telling, not showing signs. Is there any overwriting that tells too much at the expense of showing, which hinders the emotional charge in the scene? Are the readers told how to feel about a certain event or character at any point? If there are, it's time to start editing.

Achieving the best setting for your characters

You simply don't need to use an extraordinary setting for every single one of your scenes – unless you're writing sci-fi or fantasy – but please don't start your novel with your protagonist waking up in the morning in her bed and then take us all the way through her breakfast for the first five pages. Don't take us through an unbearably long dinner scene with no relevance to plot or characterisation. Don't take us on a bus ride just as an excuse to describe the setting of the whole bus route, if nothing will ever happen on this route.

These are all common shortcomings in new writing. Setting is a big deal only if you make it so. Otherwise, place it where it belongs: in the background.

Another particularly common bad habit in new writing is describing a setting that the readers would be so familiar with, they wouldn't need any descriptions. Remember the example in *Pacing your story* (page 44) about Hannah taking forever to get off the couch and find her mobile in her handbag?

Here's a similar one:

> The railway station was crowded and noisy. People moved
> about, queuing for tickets or attending to their children.
> Trains were coming and going without interruption. Ticket
> controllers, in their uniforms, were making their way through
> the masses of passengers and into the trains.

There is absolutely no point in wasting readers' time with this description, which can go on for pages and pages. This is like saying *they sat at the table, which had four legs and a board on top of them, on which the dishes were placed.* It's a great idea to use familiar settings because, in doing so, you can rely on readers' familiarity to understand and contribute to your scene with their own imagination and memory, but only if you are going to use the familiarity of the scene to present something extraordinary and you have the sense not to describe them in detail. In any case, don't spend too much time describing familiar scenes. In the above example, using the words 'railway station' should suffice since each one of your readers is likely to know what a railway station looks like and who populates it.

In fact, this principle of not wasting readers' time with descriptions of everyday settings can also extend to objects. I had a manuscript where Christmas crackers were described in two long paragraphs, and a third one summed the previous two up with, 'so basically they look like large toffees and they contain a small object as a surprise.' Fragments like this are the easiest to just delete forever without the worry that your story will be affected in any way.

Keep this in mind as you edit your manuscript scene by scene, looking at the *purpose* each scene serves. Does it move the story forward? Does it deepen a character more? If it doesn't, it's just a padding, a random scene that could be replaced easily with any other scene with no adverse effect whatsoever.

However, when built properly, any scene has the potential to tell us something about characters. A dinner scene, one of the most familiar scenes to any reader, can add great depth to characters. Just remember not to waste our time with the description of porcelain, cutlery and tablecloth, unless it is absolutely relevant (e.g. to the social status of the host).

Monotony

Read your manuscript once over with scenes only in mind. Keep an eye out for *monotony* this time. You might notice that all your settings are overly familiar. You might notice that your story takes place in the same setting for a long time or for the whole length of it.

In that case, readers are likely to forget your story and your characters really easily. It's time to change things and make your scenes more memorable. It's time to give readers a wake-up shake-up by either moving your story to a fresh setting or by speeding up the pace.

Example

Jim and Hannah have another routine conversation over dinner. She shows him even more babygros she bought earlier, but she notices that Jim is reserved and distant. Hannah starts getting contractions and the setting is changed from the dining table to inside the car, stuck in traffic on a bridge, about ten miles from the hospital, Hannah in agony and Jim petrified of not making it to the hospital in time. That's when he tells her that, once the baby is born, he wants a divorce.

This is likely to wake your readers up, right? Now imagine Jim breaking the divorce news to Hannah in the dining room, while she's going through the babygros. The difference lies in keeping the monotony of your scenes and settings or breaking it.

The car scene works better because it alerts the readers and because it's more memorable.

However, don't overkill your story with shocking scenes one after another. That's why the following exercise is intended to help you plan and revise your scenes so they have a greater impact on your readers.

Exercise

Get a large Post-It block. Go through your manuscript carefully and write a brief description of your scenes, one scene per Post-It. Arrange your scenes chronologically on the wall in front of you.

What do you notice? Are your scenes:

+ in the same setting all the time or for a long period of time;

+ written in the same pace;

+ alternating action, description and reflection;

+ introducing a fresh new setting when readers need a wake-up warning, there's important stuff ahead;

+ evoking the right atmosphere;

+ achieving their purpose (i.e. developing character, moving the story forward, slowing the story down etc)?

6 Elements of copy-editing and basic copy preparation

You're finished. You added that last full stop and wrote The End. Congratulations! The hundreds of hours of writing and the thousands of hours reading, rewriting and editing are done with and you're free.

Except that there is one last task to do. No self-respecting self-editing book is going to overlook the all-important task of *copy-editing*.

If you're going to send your manuscript to an agent or publisher, all you have to do is present it nicely, according to their submission guidelines (see Chapter 7 for details on how to present your manuscript to agents and publishers).

But if you're looking to self-publish to industry standards, you will deal directly with a copy-editor, a typesetter, a proofreader and a cover designer at least. Therefore in this chapter, you will find a brief introduction to basic copy preparation. Use it to familiarise yourself with the prepress process – the long road a manuscript takes to turn into a book – and the main terminology.

Understanding the different roles of *development editor* and *copy-editor*

Before a manuscript is typeset into a book, it is still a *copy*, hence the term *copy-editing*. Contrary to some beliefs, a *copy-editor's* job is different from a *development editor's* job. A copy-editor's task is not to develop your manuscript at the level of content, i.e. plot, narrative, characterisation, scenes and setting, or writing style. This is a development editor's job. I use the term development editor loosely here, as borrowed from non-fiction, where development editors, usually specialists in the book's subject matter, will read the manuscript in order to offer suggestions on how to develop it further. For fiction, a development editor is commonly called a *literary consultant*. Literary consultants are usually published fiction authors themselves or independent fiction editors. They will read a manuscript and prepare an assessment report at the content level, making achievable suggestions and helping the author realise the most of the story's potential.

A copy-editor's task is a lot more technical than this. It refers mainly to formatting and style, but it will include editing for clarity and consistency.

What does a copy-editor do?

A copy-editor's main task is to prepare the copy for typesetting. The copy-editor will code each part of the copy in specific codes and mark up the body of the text with these codes, so the typesetter knows what style to apply to different parts of the texts. For fiction, the two main codes will be specific fonts and styles for chapter headings and paragraphs. But, for instance, if there are fragments of text that need to stand out, such as an SMS message, it might require a different font.

A copy-editor will standardise the whole body of the book so the typesetter knows what everything should look like at any given point, he or she will correct spelling, punctuation, sentence structure and will raise queries about specific uses of grammar with the author. The copy-editor will improve clarity and consistency where they are lacking and will check closely with the author to ensure the correct meaning appears in the final copy. He or she will also check for any legal liabilities in the text, such as sexist or racist or any type of discriminatory language, libel or infringement on the copyright and confirm with the author permissions for quotations are clear.

In non-fiction, it's common practice to quote short fragments from other authors without permission, as they would be classed as 'fair dealing' or 'fair use' and used for educational or informative purposes.

However, with fiction, it's not always the case. I found that authors feel at liberty to quote full-size poems and song lyrics in novels submitted to our consultancy. This is not usually permitted and permission forms should be submitted with the copyright holders in every case.

If you use real people or real businesses or organisations in your novel or short story, be very careful about *defamation*. Defamation is exposing someone to hatred, ridicule, contempt or injuring their reputation through libel (written defamatory statement).

If you use real settings, using real names for shops and other businesses will only add to the realism of your book and, most of the time, the organisations will be happy to see their names mentioned in a book. But it helps to point it out to them before the book is published and give them a chance to tell you how they feel about it. If they express discomfort (at having their place described as a gruesome murder scene, for example), be considerate and go for a fictional alternative.

After copy-editing, the copy goes for typesetting.

What does a typesetter do?

A typesetter will design the internal layout of the book. The copy will be paginated and stylised into book-shape, containing *leaves*, each side of which is called a *page*. The pages on the left hand side of the spread (or opening) are called *verso* and are numbered in even numbers, the pages on the right hand side are called *recto*, and are numbered in odd numbers.

What does a proofreader do?

Once it's been typeset, the manuscript becomes a *proof.* Hence the term *proofreading.* This is a common confusion among unpublished writers. Some of our clients come to us and say, 'I need to have my manuscript proofread.' You can't have a manuscript proofread. You can have it copy-edited, which includes checking for grammar and punctuation errors. We understand what they mean, as anyone else would, but using the appropriate jargon in conversation with a publisher can add to your credibility.

A proofreader will check the typesetter did a good job, by checking the proof against the copy to ensure no *matter* – the term for any part of the copy's content – has been left out. The proofreader will also check for presentation errors – such as bad hyphenation, widows and orphans, where lines are left hanging at the end or the beginning of a new page, and for non-fiction, figures, tables, captions, cross-references and indexing are correctly laid out and accurate, as well as the consistency of style, i.e. if all chapter headings and paragraphs are set in their respective font and style throughout.

The proofreader will mark the proof in BSI – the British Standard for marking copy – and it will go back to the typesetter, where the corrections will be made.

Ideally, it should be read once again at this stage for any oversights before it's *ready for print* or *passed for press* or *signed off.*

Understanding and complying with house style

The way a book is copy-edited and designed, the style and fonts chosen will depend on a house style – the publisher presents the team comprising the copy-editor, the typesetter and the proofreader with a style list, a specific way in which the book will be prepared for print. Small publishing houses may have a single house style for all their titles, but it's common practice for bigger houses to have a unique style per author and sometimes per series or even for standalone titles.

We can talk freely about *rules* here, not just advice, because copy preparation is regulated in the English-speaking publishing world by two main canons: *The Oxford Style for British English* and *The Chicago Style for American English.* At Daniel Goldsmith Associates, we also use *Style Manual: For Authors, Editors and Printers* for Australian and New Zealand clients.

It's very unusual for an author looking to publish his or her own books to create a complete house style. What we usually do is talk to the author about the way in which some of the competitor titles, i.e. successful titles in the same genre, have been designed and stylised and the author usually chooses a favourite. We don't copy it, we suggest similar styles until we reach an agreement.

Getting to grips with grammar, punctuation, spelling, clarity and concision

Pay particular attention to these common mistakes:

Which or that?

Use *which* in non-restrictive clauses, where one clause doesn't modify the other, as in, '*This table, which is missing a leg, will have to do*' and *that* in restrictive clauses, where one clause modifies the other, as in, '*I found a table that is missing a leg*'.

Me or I?

I is the indicative form of the pronoun, thus the *subject* of the verb's action, whereas *me* is the accusative/dative form, thus the recipient of the verb's action. Put simply, when subject, *I* do the action. When object, the action is done to *me*. That's why is not correct to say 'Hannah and me went to the market', because if it wasn't for 'Hannah and', we wouldn't say 'Me went to the market'.

Subject–pronoun agreement

In order to avoid sexist language, some writers choose to use a neutral plural pronoun when referring to a singular noun. For example, 'if the baby gets out of the car seat, it's important that they are returned to it immediately'. This is grammatically incorrect, however the practice is so widespread that it doesn't seem to cause too much bother any more.

Subject–verb agreement

When you refer to a collective noun as one entity, correct noun–verb agreement is to use the verb in the singular, as in, '*The Police has announced new measures for crime prevention*', but when you use the singular noun as multiple entities, use the verb in the plural, as in, '*The police have taken their seats.*'

Who, whom, whose

Who is the interrogative form, *whom* the accusative form (i.e. the object of a verb), *whose* is the possessive form (belongs to a noun).

Misused apostrophes

Probably the most recurrent grammar mistake in new writing is using the apostrophe to form the plural form. The apostrophe is *never* used to form plurals. It has two main functions: to form a contraction, as in '*It's raining today*', where *it is* has been contracted to *it's*, and to indicate possession, as in, 'Jim's car broke down.'

'Odd' words, such as words ending in vowels, e.g. portfolio, video, mama etc., don't need the apostrophe to form their plural either. Decades, like the 1990s, 1970s, the 2000s don't need one either.

Dangling modifiers

'*Stepping outside, the bus arrived just in time.*' It's obvious that here it's not the bus that stepped outside, although the way the sentence is constructed, it leaves the modifying sentence 'dangling'.

Homophones

The commonest confusions are *you're/your, their/there/they're*.

The full stop

I was bemused to discover that most American clients leave a double space after a full stop (they call it a period). You, British, American, Australian or any other English-speaker, shouldn't do this. It's not correct practice in America and it certainly isn't in Britain either, so always leave single space after a full stop. In order to check if you have any repeated spaces in your manuscript, use the Find and Replace tool in Word and type ' ' (click spacebar twice) in Find and ' ' (single click on spacebar) in Replace and Word will replace all occurrences throughout your manuscript. You can also do it manually in Paragraph view, wherever you see two space dots instead of one.

Single or double quotation marks?

It's a British thing to use single quote marks, however, it has become more of a personal choice lately. My personal choice for electronic editions are the double quotes as they give dialogue higher visibility on screen, which increases vividness.

Dialogue lines always start a new paragraph. An exception is when the speaker is the subject of the preceding narrative; in this case, the dialogue line can follow the narrative line immediately.

Example
Jim scratched his forehead. 'Hmm, I'm not sure about this.'

and not

Jim scratched his forehead.

'Hmm, I'm not sure about this.'

If the publisher's house style requires otherwise, the copy-editor will change it anyway.

Serial exclamation marks

What can be more annoying than an exclamation mark every paragraph or so? That's right, two or more exclamation marks at the end of the sentence. Come on. One (or more) exclamation mark(s) will not turn an unexciting sentence into an exciting one. This is valid for punctuation in general. Think of punctuation in terms of utility, not style. Use a more precise word instead of an exclamation mark to get the right message across and don't bully your readers with serial exclamation marks.

All caps

Talking about bullying your readers, nothing does a better job than SHOUTING in text, does it? All caps are likely to be found in some dialogue, where volume is intended. If you really have to, use a single exclamation mark. Otherwise, work harder to find a more subtle way of suggesting it and never use all caps, unless for abbreviations and other acceptable uses.

Clarity

The brief here is to make this text clearer:

Example
Jim advanced and looked the CEO in the eye. He provided

him with the long-awaited report. The point that he wanted to make was that there was no need for this type of behaviour from a superior. He estimated roughly that he was being treated contemptuously by his boss on a daily basis.

My revision:

Jim got closer and looked the CEO in the eye. He gave him the report. There was no need for this type of behaviour from a superior, Jim thought. His boss treats him contemptuously every day.

This type of editing is called *substantive editing*. It involves a lot of rewriting and rewording and it's very unusual in editing fiction. But because you're editing your own writing, you can allow yourself unlimited amounts of substantive editing in order to make your writing clearer.

Concision

The brief here is to revise this fragment in order to improve concision:

Example

Hannah watched the single envelope fall slowly through the letterbox in the door and land on the mat with a soft thud. She noticed the yellow stamp in the right top corner and knew straight away. Jim had had his solicitor write her a letter to file for divorce.

This is my revision:

Hannah watched the envelope fall through the letterbox and land on the mat. She noticed the yellow stamp and knew straight away. Jim had filed for divorce.

The letterbox is always in the door. The location of the stamp is neither here nor there. Mentioning 'solicitor' in the same sentence as 'divorce' is not only predictable and dull, but it breaks the punchiness of the sentence too. A shorter sentence will deliver a greater punch in this case. It is a crucial moment for Hannah – realising her husband will divorce her. No need to clutter the emotional impact on the reader with verbiage.

Getting published 7

I know you come to publishing with low or no expectations for the financial side. You know writing is the lowest paid activity you'll probably ever undertake. Still, it never mattered and it never should. This is likely to be controversial with a lot of people. Many successful authors and publishing professionals would energetically disagree here, advising you never to accept second-best, but in your heart you know publishing success for you would not be just about money. You write because you have something to say. You have a story to tell and you know there are people who would benefit from reading it. They might be in their hundreds, they might be in their millions, it really doesn't make a difference in your choice to write or stop writing.

I remember Eddie Bell, a reputable agent from the Bell Lomax Moreton Agency, saying at a conference during the 2010 London Book Fair that, 'New fiction is pretty much a closed shop in the UK.' I don't think things have changed much since 2010 – rather, I think it's getting increasingly more difficult for new writers to break through and get published.

Still, it's not impossible and, with a clear focus and a bit of planning, you can approach the getting published battle in an intelligent and effective way, as opposed to the desperate and bitter way, which is the only other way.

At Daniel Goldsmith Associates, we run a nationwide series of workshops on getting published. In these full-day workshops, we talk to delegates about publishing statistics, we try to establish what they would define as *success* for themselves as writers and we try to work out an *action plan* or *road map* to navigate to this success.

Making an action plan

The plans are always individual, but they all have common points or milestones. These points are:

1. **Make sure your work is as ready as can be before you present it to any agent or publisher**. How can you do this? Reading this book is a significant step towards achieving the *ready* stage. However, simply reading it won't make the difference to your manuscript. You need to do the actual revision to the best of your abilities. Once self-editing is completed, give the manuscript to the most avid readers from your circle of friends. You'll be amazed what a fresh pair of eyes can bring to your writing.

Most people have a friend who never stops reading. The friend that has every inch of wall covered with book shelves. The friend who pays extra for luggage allowance to take just 11 more paperbacks on her or his weekend away. This is the one to pester first. Friends and family can provide invaluable feedback at the early stages of the self-editing process. They can flag up a plot inconsistency, such as, 'Hang on, how come Jim says in Chapter Eight that the accident happened at

midday, when it was on the nine o'clock news in Chapter One?'
Great bit of spotting from good old uncle George. Imagine the
embarrassment if this flag-up appeared in a review after you
published the book.

Joining a writing group, an evening class or an online course can
prove very useful too. Here people meet other like-minded writers,
make friends, get feedback on their writing and learn skills they can
take home and use in their own writing. To find out more and
register for a workshop in your area, please check
www.danielgoldmith.co.uk/workshops.php.

The Arvon Foundation in England runs amazing workshops and
residential courses in some of the most beautiful locations around
the UK and with some A-list authors as tutors. They receive
funding from The Arts Council and can help aspiring authors with
the cost of attending the courses. Please check
www.arvonfoundation.org/courses

Once your second revision is completed, consider getting a
professional and market-aware opinion from a publishing insider,
such as an editor or a literary consultant. An editor will not only
work with you to improve your writing, but he or she will advise you
what the next step is for you and who in the industry to approach, be
it an agent or a publisher's editor. A good independent editor with
valuable industry connections may well be a writer's first open door.
Employing an editor can be costly and the fees vary from hundreds to
thousands of pounds, depending on what type of editing and what
type of editor you hire.

Harry Bingham, of *Writers' Workshop*, expresses the same opinion in
his guide, *Writers' and Artists' Yearbook Guide to Getting Published*

(2011): 'When manuscripts don't sell, when they get rejected by agents, it's almost always because the darn things were never good enough in the first place, and that in turn means that writers are sending them out prematurely.'

If professional work is financially unavailable to you, the next best step is to make a list of agents who accept unsolicited manuscripts and, preferably, offer feedback on submissions. These agents are less and less easy to find, due to the sheer volume of submissions. Even small feedback from an agent in a rejection letter can be immensely helpful.

We have a client who approached the children's literary agent, Julia Churchill, with the first three chapters of her 9–12 detective novel. The agent requested to see the whole manuscript. After reading more, she rejected it with this invaluable piece of feedback:

> *Dear Karen,*
>
> *Thank you for giving me a shot with this. It's not one for me I'm afraid. I think it's a little drawn out and busy, and the stakes aren't clear enough to keep me pulled in. No doubt you can write, and another agent may love this. But I'm being very careful about what I take on at the moment, and this doesn't quite make me jump.*
>
> *I'm sorry not to have better news for you.*
>
> *Good luck with it,*
>
> *Julia*

Because of this feedback, the author now has a clear idea of what this agent is looking for as well as what is lacking in her book. She is currently working on her manuscript and trying to make the story more straightforward in the opening chapters and raise the stakes.

So feedback from agents should be acted upon, as long as the feedback makes sense to the author and the author feels it would work well in the context.

2. **Once you feel your book is as good as it can be and you have received significant positive feedback on your manuscript, you're ready to send it out.**

Knowing your readers

Knowing your market means knowing your audience and knowing your audience means knowing what your readers will expect your book to deliver in terms of reading experience. And this is vital to the success of your novel or short story.

But knowing your market may seem easier than it is. What I have found is that most clients who are concerned about marketability and enquire about their genre and their audience look mainly in one direction: classic or very successful authors in their genre. You want to write crime, look at how the big names write. If you're writing romance, read nothing but bestsellers in the romance genre. And so on. This is certainly not a bad start. You need to read as much as you can within your genre to understand what your readers want to read.

Unfortunately, reading your genre is not enough to help you understand how to go about getting published. Efficient research means covering not only your audience, but also your channels to reach that audience, i.e. agents and publishers.

If you shouldn't look only at big names, who else should you look at? The answer is to look at which new authors big publishers have signed up last year. Or the year before. But no longer than three years ago. This research into what kind of new fiction sells and who buys it will give you a solid focus. Where you previously made no more than aimless efforts and were getting nowhere with your unpublished book, you now have a certain knowledge of what kind of books publishers are looking for and who might potentially want to hear from you.

But finding out what publishers sign up every time and especially who, out of the whole list, is a debut author, is very hard work indeed. If there were one single database of all the debut novels published every year in the UK, I would be their number one subscriber. But there isn't one, so in the meanwhile, we have to collect manually information from industry sources, such as *The Bookseller* (www.thebookseller.com) or www.booktrade.info. They both have free daily newsletters where new deals are announced all the time. Subscribing to a literary supplement, like *The Times Literary Supplement* or reading *The Guardian's* books section online will help tremendously. Subscribing to a writing magazine, such as *The Writers' Forum* or *Writing Magazine*, will come in handy too.

For readers who want to keep an eye on the American market too, *Huffington Post Books* (www.huffingtonpost.com/books), *The New York Review of Books* (www.nybooks.com), *Publishers Weekly* (www.publishersweekly.com), *Publishers Marketplace* (former *Publishers Lunch*, www.publishersmarketplace.com) and *Writer's Digest* (www.writersdigest.com).

All these websites have news feeds and free newsletters, making it easier for you to receive only news and updates, without having to go through lots of old content.

Once you start gathering information on what new fiction publishers sign on, you'll start gaining a valuable insight and you will be able to estimate your own book's chances in the current market.

Building market-awareness is difficult and time-consuming and keeping up to date is hard work, but it is *not* impossible.

As with everything else, there is a shortcut you can take by consulting a professional editor whose job is to keep up to date with the market. Literary consultants and reputable independent editors will offer market advice on most fiction manuscripts and can point you in the right direction as far as agents and publishers are concerned.

Once you become aware of your audience, the next thing on the list should be finding out accurately what this audience is likely to expect from your book. With so many books out there, audiences become more and more educated and hard to please. This can only be achieved through reading as much as you can within your genre.

So, to summarise, in order to become more market-aware, you need to do some thorough research:

1.   Read most debut novels published by large publishers in the last three years to understand what *publishers* want, and

2.   Read most of the critically acclaimed and best-selling novels within your genre to understand what your *audience* wants and expects from your book.

While reading Stephen King's *On Writing*, one thing struck me as unusual. When he was 13, not unlike teenagers in general, King wrote quite a lot of fiction. However, unlike most teenage writers, King didn't just do this for personal enjoyment and didn't leave his single-spaced manuscript in his desk drawer. He sent it to his favourite kids' sci-fi magazine. He was rejected, so he tried a different magazine. He was rejected again and again. He printed his short story on A4 sheets, drew a basic illustration on the 'cover' and sold it to his schoolmates, making a profit of a few dollars. It was going to be years and only a handful of magazine articles until *Carrie* was seen by Doubleday and he was offered a $2,500 advance.

So, from the moment Stephen King started writing, one goal had a firm grip on his mind: getting published.

Once you have a completed first draft, self-edit until you're satisfied it's as good as you could possibly make it. Once you have reached this stage, there is only one thing you can do and it's not forgetting about it.

Send your manuscript out into the world. Magazine and fiction competitions are an excellent start. You can get invaluable feedback from them and a fair idea about how your writing scores against the unpublished competition. Agents and publishers' editors are also a safe bet, but prepare to learn what patience truly is, with reply letters arriving as late as three or four months, and expect rejections. Lots of them. Literary consultants and independent editors are an easier route, if you're willing to pay for their services.

One thing I am more than happy *to guarantee* is that if there is genuine potential and value in your work you *will* be discovered. I can't stress enough how important it is to have your manuscript seen by someone even remotely connected to the industry. After all, you have invested thousands of hours in writing your manuscript and thousands of hours improving it through endless rewriting and editing, so give it a fair chance and show it to someone.

Getting feedback

As a writer and especially as a writer of fiction, you're likely to *crave* feedback. It's only natural. Exciting stories and plots take place in your world, complicated and impossible quests are resolved by amazing characters. It's nothing if not worth talking about.

How to approach a literary agent

Presenting your manuscript to a literary agent can be an unnerving plan. It's all a big worry. Is it the right agent, the right letter, the right synopsis, the right number of pages submitted?

Do you need an agent?

If you write fiction, you do need an agent. For non-fiction writers, a well-crafted book proposal will attract an editor's attention equally if submitted by an agent or directly by the author.

However, things are a little more complicated with fiction and this is mainly due to the overwhelming number of submissions editors would receive without the added benefit of an extra curator – the literary agent.

What does a literary agent do?

Put simply, an agent is a writer's business partner. A writer is the creative engine and so he or she should remain, once an agent deals with the business side. Agents approach publishers, negotiate deals and royalty rates. They represent their clients at international book fairs where they sell translation rights to overseas publishers. They approach TV or film producers and negotiate adaptation deals.

Any writer, new or established, will benefit immensely from working with an agent, so the ten or 15 per cent commission agents retain on sales shouldn't put anyone off.

You are more likely to get published if you're a new author and you are offered representation by an established and reputable agent. Agents and editors work on first-name terms. If an editor receives a manuscript from an agent he or she knows and has previously worked with, it's quite likely they will give it a lot of attention.

But no one knows *everyone*. That's why you need to choose agents carefully.

How to choose a literary agent

The excellent directory *Writers' and Artists' Yearbook* is your first port of call. It has a large list of agents, each with a small description and often with a list of clients. Go through the list carefully and select a few names and address *based on their portfolio*.

Why based on their portfolio? Because, if they successfully placed books similar to yours with publishers, this means that they know editors who will be interested in your kind of book. Agents can dial editors on their personal extension numbers and tell them they've got a hot book for them. If an agent hasn't placed anything in your genre yet, move on.

You should now concentrate on the list you compiled. To shorten your long list, do some basic internet research into each agency. The info on each agency's website will give you a better clue of what the agent or agents are like, what they are looking for and whether they accept unsolicited manuscripts.

For now, approach only agents who welcome unsolicited manuscripts, according to their submission guidelines. If an agent requires exclusivity, you have two options:

+ approach only the particular agent, or

+ delay approaching him or her until you have received a response from other agents who are happy to receive simultaneous submissions.

This process can be time consuming and the waiting game can be nerve-wracking. There are no statistics for how long literary agents take to reply. Some of them specify the response time on their website, but if you haven't received a reply within three months, assume rejection and move on.

However, you simply need to select agents and have a very basic knowledge of who might be interested in your book. We sometimes get enquiries in the shape of, 'I'm a British author, I've written a political thriller based in the USA and I'm not sure which agent to approach. Can you help with a few names?' OK. Give me the next two full days and I'll have the list.

Example

A client was seeking representation for her literary novel. She felt her writing was closer to Anne Enright's and logically assumed that people who liked Anne Enright's writing would like her writing too. She found out that Anne Enright's agent is Gill Coleridge of Rogers Coleridge & White. The agency accepts unsolicited submissions, so she sent a covering letter, the synopsis and the first 50 pages, as advised on the agency's website. She addressed her letter to Gill Coleridge personally and mentioned that it's because of the similarity with Anne Enright's writing, that our client believed Gill Coleridge would make the ideal agent.

This is a good way to approach an agent. Still, within a few weeks, the author received a standard rejection letter. The book simply didn't stand out enough in today's competitive market.

But, while doing her research, our client also found out that Lucy Luck, a newer London agent, also worked with Anne Enright, as an agent's editorial assistant. So she approached Lucy Luck, who already has a superb literary list and who also accepts unsolicited submissions. Our client is currently waiting for a response.

This is a very efficient and accurate way of finding a suitable agent. Think of an author you feel particularly close to and find out who his or her agent is. A basic search on the internet will give you all the information you need. You need to know *who* to approach as well as *how* to approach them. If you do your research properly and in an intelligent way, you will waste less time and money on printing and posting pointless submissions to the wrong agents.

How to prepare your submission

Once you have shortlisted a few agents you feel confident about, visit their websites one by one and write down their submission guidelines. Agents can be pedantic in the extreme. They hate typos, poor spelling and poor grammar in a deeply disturbing and personal way. Here's the proof, in the words of Katie Green, former literary scout and literary agency assistant:

> *Every author thinks that their manuscript is special and unique. And of course, for them it is. For agents, however, it's a different story. Visit any agency and one of the first things you'll see is a pile of jiffy bags a foot high, all containing unsolicited submissions. Many agencies get over a hundred submissions a month. It takes a huge amount of time to wade through them all, so it's important to make sure that your submission catches the agent's attention for the right, rather than the wrong, reasons. The first thing they read is the covering letter so it's important to get this right. The covering letter is not the place to show off how wacky or creative you are. It is essentially a business letter so it should be businesslike. And brief. And containing all the relevant information as specified in the submission guidelines. (By the way, always follow the guidelines. They are there for a reason.) And most definitely error-free – if you can't manage to correctly spell, punctuate and type a brief letter, it does not bode well for the rest of the submission and the agent will already come to it with lowered expectations. If the pile of submissions is particularly high, they might be tempted to simply move on to the next without reading a word of your story (harsh, but possible). So check, check, and check again. And then again. The truth is, agents approach their unsolicited submissions with a great deal of hope, but massively low expectations. Receiving a good submission is a joy – another*

bad one is simply annoying. Make sure yours is a good one or it will be going straight into the reject pile, spelling mistakes and all.

The query letter

When the agent doesn't welcome unsolicited submissions, this means that he or she does not wish to receive your manuscript, not even the first three chapters, or, if they receive it, they will not be able to look at it or reply to you about your submission.

It's better not to send unsolicited submissions, as they will be discarded as soon as they're received, and you'd just be wasting your time and money.

The way to approach agents who don't receive unsolicited submissions is to send them a *query letter*.

A query letter is a letter of interest in which you invite the agent to solicit your manuscript.

Example of a good query letter

Dear Hannah Smith,

I am seeking representation for my first novel, 'If Only for an Hour'.

'If Only for an Hour' is the story of Adam, an ordinary guy in his late thirties who falls in love with another man. Adam is married and, when his wife falls ill, Adam has to face an agonising guilt as he starts planning to leave her and start a new life with the one person he feels he truly loves.

The novel is complete at 80,000 words. I feel quite close to Adam Parker's writing from your list, hence you are the only agent I have contacted so far. I am 40 years old and I live in Yorkshire with my wife, a long-time sufferer of MS.

Please find enclosed a self-addressed stamped envelope for your reply. I am happy to wait for your reply before I approach another agent.

Yours sincerely,

Jim Hopeful

As with all the examples in this book, this is also based on real submissions. You must recognise the subtlety and elegance in approach of this query letter. It's not in the agent's face by any means, but still very much to the point. When the author adds his age and the detail of living with his wife, who suffers from multiple sclerosis, we get it that the story could be based on his own experience. This is intriguing and encouraging as far as the author's ability to suggest is concerned. It also shows a certain confidence in the reader's ability to understand from suggestions, a rare encounter in beginning writers.

Example of a bad query letter

Dear Agent,

My name is Jim Hopeful and I have written an 80,000-word novel on homosexual love titled IF ONLY FOR AN HOUR. I am currently looking for an agent to represent the book and my future books.

When his wife falls ill, Adam plans to leave her and move in with another man, who he realises he truly loves. IF ONLY FOR AN HOUR is the story of how he copes with the guilt of being in love with someone else when his wife needs him most.

I am 40 years old and I live in Yorkshire with my wife. Adam's story is based on my personal experience, rendering it an authenticity the LGBT (lesbian, gay, bisexual, transgender) community of readers will recognise and appreciate.

I am available for contact at the above details. Adam Parker is one of my favourite authors, therefore Hannah Smith Agency was my first choice. I would highly appreciate a speedy reply, this would allow me to approach other agents who might be interested in representing IF ONLY FOR AN HOUR.

Yours sincerely,

Jim Hopeful

By contrast, this example is pretty bad. There is no subtlety at all. The message is made loud and clear. Unless this is a specialist LGBT agent, by mentioning the LGBT audience the author actually narrows his chances. He uses all caps for the title instead of inverted single commas, which is the recommended style for unpublished titles, giving his letter an unappealingly eager tone.

The covering letter

Most agents will require a covering letter with your manuscript and synopsis. A good covering letter tells them a bit about the book and about yourself. My first piece of advice is not to make it too informal; it tends to get annoying after a few of them. Don't tell the agent, 'I've seen your portfolio and I've read on a blog that you like Shakespeare, so I think we would get on well.' Don't tell the agent, 'I do the writing, you do the selling and we're cool.' It's a general assumption that this is exactly how things work, no need to tell the agent how to do his or her job.

Don't address the agent as 'Dear Sirs' or 'Dear Gentlemen'. It's very likely a woman will read the letter and this makes for an extremely bad start.

At our literary consultancy, we offer a free service in which we copy-edit covering letters from new authors. Here's an example of a good covering letter amassed from multiple submissions.

Example of a good covering letter

Dear Hannah Smith,

I am seeking representation for my novel, 'If Only for an Hour', a love story on finding true love and losing it due to society pressure and an overly conservative upbringing. In many ways, this is my story. The protagonist's quest — to find true happiness with a same-sex partner — or spend the rest of his life living unhappily with his wife — is my own quest. Writing the book has helped me find the answer to what I ultimately want from life and the huge amount I need to sacrifice in order to achieve it.

Adam Parker is one of my favourite authors and the fact that he is on your list makes me think there is no other agent better suited for my book.

Please find enclosed the synopsis and the first three chapters according to your submission guidelines.

Yours sincerely,

Jim Hopeful

This example is closely based on a real covering letter I received. I instantly liked it. I felt it worked really well. Not too pushy, not long, not too personal, but personal enough to intrigue about the authenticity of this story.

Example of a bad covering letter

Dear Sirs,

My name is Jim Hopeful and I am submitting the first three chapters of my novel, IF ONLY FOR AN HOUR, for your valued attention. IF ONLY FOR AN HOUR is a gay romance story on the timeless theme of finding The Special One and then losing them due to unforeseen circumstances. I would consider myself, as a writer, in the same category as Jackie Collins, but with the added benefit of a male's perspective over seduction and love.

I am a mechanical engineer, currently working for myself in the renewable energy sector, I've been writing for over eight months now and I feel I'm ready to approach a publisher. I've been advised by an industry insider to approach an agent first to negotiate a better deal with the publisher.

I would highly appreciate if you could consider approaching Mills and Boon and Simon and Schuster, as they seem to publish mainly the type of books I write. I am looking for a business partnership with an agent. A business partnership in which all I have to do is write and get on with my very busy job and the agent represents my interests. I am not interested primarily in making money, although I obviously wouldn't turn it away if it were to come my way.

I'm available to travel to London for a meeting (maybe over lunch?), where we can discuss a possible sequel I have in mind, at your convenience.

Yours truly,

Jim Hopeful, PE (Professional Engineer)

So, where do we start?

The first noticeable thing is that almost every sentence starts with 'I', with the exception of one sentence is that it starts with 'my'. The two-line description of the book by its theme is uninteresting and entirely unintriguing. The sentences are structured in the same way, the standard subject – verb – object, showing complete lack of creativity and resulting in a very dull letter. Clichés abound, such as 'for your valued attention' (we can almost see the agent's eyes fluttering with delight) or 'due to unforeseen circumstances' (hardly anyone's eyes would ping with interest at this cliché).

Dull, if it wasn't for the attitude of the letter, of course. The author compares himself with a hugely successful author in the romance genre. Comparisons like this *never* work, so resist them.

The information about the author's profession and industry is irrelevant; the author is proposing a romance novel, not a manual on solar panels maintenance. 'An industry insider' sounds presumptuous and inappropriate when talking to *the* ultimate industry insider, so please, please resist them too.

In fact the letter gets more and more presumptuous as it goes on. I can't imagine which agent would have enough time and nerve to read it until the end. Obviously, you shouldn't make publisher suggestions in your covering letter to a literary agent. It might sound like a good idea to do a bit of their job for them, since they are so busy, but no, it really is a bad one.

The suggestion to meet over lunch is quite cute. I can almost see the agent cooing and awing over it and then looking in her agenda only to notice that her lunch slots are sadly all booked.

And the agent is based in Edinburgh. And she is a woman.

Oh, and mentioning you're not after money with this book? Not what a literary agent would like to hear.

On the feeble good side, the covering letter is no longer than one page, so well done, Jim Hopeful, on getting that right.

When writing a letter to a stranger, you really need to keep a neutral attitude to be on the safe side. Don't paint all your walls in Funky Colours Matt Lollipops just before you put your house up for sale. Not everybody likes Matt Lollipops. However, if you have one buyer you believe is the ideal buyer for your house and you have found out he or she owns several other houses, all painted in different shades of Matt Lollipops, then go ahead, impress them.

If you have one agent in mind, a basic research on the internet about the agent's list, any interviews, articles or talks they have given will help you in getting a feel about what the agent is looking for. Entries in the *Writers' and Artists' Yearbook* are all pretty generic, they give little away about the agent's taste and personality.

Synopsis

For some unknown reason, writing a synopsis seems to be one of those things that should be straightforward by nature but are overly complicated by method. Many clients come to us for help, worried that their synopsis and not the manuscript, is responsible for agents' rejection. This is nothing more than a myth.

I think writers worry about this mainly because they believe a synopsis needs *to pitch* the book to the agent or editor instead of simply *outlining* it. So they worry about tone (is it too pushy?) and the content (is it too long? does it cover enough?).

Let's make it clear that the synopsis is *not* a back cover blurb for your book. It doesn't need to tease the reader and it certainly doesn't need to intrigue as far as the story is concerned. The purpose of the synopsis is the exact opposite: it needs to make the story clear and easy to understand and follow in three pages or fewer.

It really doesn't take much effort to write a synopsis as long as you keep it simple and to the point. What happens in the story? Answer this question by outlining the main events, describing as you go the main characters in no more than 1,000 words (i.e. three pages). Talk briefly about the theme of the novel, if there is a set one, perhaps right at the beginning, include the ending and you're done.

Although I have seen different advice, I personally prefer synopses that tell the story, the twist and the ending in full. If I were an agent, I would like to know the ending without having to spend the rest of the week reading the whole manuscript. All the agents I know prefer this.

If you choose otherwise, resist the urge to tease the agent with something like, '. . . and if you wish to know how it all ends, read it.' This is an instant killer.

The synopsis doesn't have to have a full list of characters and certainly no description for every one of them.

Example of a good synopsis

The Crash

'The Crash' is a corporate thriller depicting the greediness and irresponsibility of an investment bank using illegal methods to cover up an increasing amount of debt upon which large investment portfolios are based.

Jim McIntyre is a financial executive for a major investment bank. He lives in the heart of the City and spends most of his life in the office, at the expense of his wife and three-year-old twin daughters who seldom see him.

As investments start to fail one by one, Jim starts to receive confidential orders from his superiors to cover the size of the damage in order to minimise panic amongst investment clients. A two million pound bonus is promised for the end of the year if Jim can cover the disaster. Left on his own with the executive team distancing further away from him every day for fear of not bearing any responsibility if the truth is found out, Jim is feeling more and more isolated and left to take decisions for himself.

As his marriage is breaking down and his PA tells him

she's pregnant with his child, Jim gets deeper into deceit, so complicated it's impossible to escape it. As one of the bank's clients with a large portfolio of investments starts to fear that something is going wrong there when, due to a basic procedure error, the bank fails to liquidify one of his assets, Jim decides that borrowing more is the only way to save appearances.

He starts falsifying documents so figures show in the bank's favour with other investors and for a while things seem to get back to normal. He gets his two million dollar bonus and, due to a loop in the contract, leaves the bank and runs away to Brazil, where he tries to get a new identity.

The fraud is revealed, the bank crashes with none of the executives accepting responsibility for the fraud. An international manhunt is set up for Jim by Scotland Yard's fraud department.

Jim is sentenced to 40 years and, while being escorted to his cell, he asks to call his wife and his PA. The two million pounds had been deposited in two anonymous bank accounts in Switzerland, one for his wife and one for his PA.

There is scope for a sequel, in the action thriller genre, concerning Jim escaping prison with the help of an American criminal and hunting down the bank executives responsible for ruining his life one by one.

The novel contains 85,000 words.

Example of a bad synopsis

The Crash

'The Crash' is a fast-paced, tense, intelligent and thought-provoking thriller with a very contemporary topic.

Jim McIntyre is a high-flyer City executive who works very late every day and has an affair with his PA, although he has a wife and twin daughters.

It's 2008 and investments start to fail one by one, adding enormous pressure on Jim's bosses to save the bank from bankruptcy, which is what would happen if they cover the damage with their investment clients.

Jim is ordered to cover everything up and, while his bosses shy away from taking any major decisions, Jim is facing more and more disaster and starts borrowing astronomical amounts of money to keep appearances of normality and wealth. He commits fraud by changing figures on statements when he applies for credit from other banks and soon it's clear that this is an inescapable situation for Jim.

In the meanwhile, his wife files for divorce and his PA breaks the news to him that she is expecting his child.

A two-million pound bonus, which he has been promised if he manages to cover the scandal up, is paid to him at the end of the year and he runs away to Brazil.

The fraud is uncovered, the bank goes bankrupt, but the executives blame it all on the runaway Jim.

I have decided not to reveal the ending, as I don't want to spoil your reading experience. It is a very satisfying ending indeed, which will leave readers wanting more.

Being a novel on basically the economic meltdown, I believe 'The Crash' will appeal to a very large audience of readers who share a disdain for irresponsible and callous financiers who have brought the world to collapse.

I am currently working on a sequel in which Jim escapes prison and starts hunting down his ex-bosses one by one.

These two synopses have the same amount of information about this fictional story. However, the first one reads better, doesn't it? It's well put together, the story is presented in the order of its development. The second one, on the other hand, is muddled up, there is no chronological order in the way the story is outlined, it uses a highly colloquial style of approach and overdramatic language and pitches heavily on the merits of the book.

It's the agent or editor and only they who should decide whether the manuscript has merit or not, whether it might leave readers wanting more or not, whether the book will appeal to a large audience or not.

Manuscript

Before preparing your submission, make sure you follow the agent's guidelines for submissions, listed in the *Writers' and Artists' Yearbook* under the agency's entry, or on the agency's website. If the agent belongs to the endangered species of agents 'open to submissions', the guidelines will usually ask for a short covering letter, a synopsis and the first three chapters or the first 30–50 pages (approximately, up to a natural stop). However, I can't stress enough how important it is to follow the specific agent's guidelines. By doing so, you not only show that the approach is individual and that you value the agent, but also that you have a professional and serious attitude as opposed to the 'what the heck, they'll love it anyway' attitude, surprisingly frequent in submitting manuscripts.

However, in many cases these guidelines will say 'no unsolicited manuscripts'. In this case, resist sending the whole manuscript or even the first three chapters. Send a query letter instead. You might feel that Agent A should read your manuscript dead or alive, because you strongly believe there is no one else in the world who would connect better with your writing. However, if the agent specifies 'no unsolicited manuscripts', this simply means 'no unsolicited manuscripts will ever be read'. Not even the first page, not even the covering letter. Nothing. So move on.

Why did one, two, three, 58 agents reject your manuscript?

Unfortunately, rejections will be inevitable in your route to getting published. When you receive a rejection, this could be either because

+ your work isn't good enough

+ there is no market for a book such as yours

+ the agent doesn't have a close network he or she could sell the book to.

These three reasons are completely independent from each other so the only genuine consolation for any rejected writer could be that the agent doesn't know anyone yet who would be willing to publish the book.

The most common reason is, however, that the manuscript is just not good or valuable enough.

We had a client who came to us out of sheer desperation. He had sent his manuscript to 58 different agents and, when he got a reply, it was always a rejection. My heart sank when I read this in the covering letter. For anyone else, this would be a firm message to give up and move on to other things. Not for a writer though. It's always amazing how powerful the urge to tell a story becomes when you have a story you believe in.

Any feedback received from agents is precious. If an agent liked your work, they are likely to tell you in their rejection letter (see Julia Churchill's rejection email in *Making an action plan* on page 130).

Approaching publishers' editors directly

As a fiction writer, it would be immensely difficult for you to find a publisher directly. It's a lot easier for non-fiction authors to do so.

What are editors looking for?

Above all else, I'm after originality. This could be originality of voice, character, style or idea. If an author or agent can get this across in the opening couple of pages of a novel, then I'm hooked. I also like agents and authors who've bothered to come up with a movie/TV pitch log line, by which I mean a mini-pitch, no more than a couple of sentences, that fully communicates what the book's got going for it. If someone gets this message right, it can run right through from editorial, to sales and marketing, to the bookseller advising a prospective reader on why they should buy this book.

(Emlyn Rees, *commissioning editor at ExhibitA, the crime list at Angry Robot*)

Because I am the only commissioning editor at Aston Bay Press, Aston Bay's list is a highly personal choice. My choices are a combination of rational and impulsive choices. I chose Joanna Price's Kate Linton series because of its contemporaneity, a rare thing in British mystery fiction, and because of the sheer wit and originality with which it is written. I love the characters too, especially Brown. When an editor and an agent enthused over it too, the urge to publish it became so powerful, I started losing sleep over it and it would be the last thing I would think about at night and the first I would think about in the morning. I had to start Aston Bay Press to publish the Kate Linton Series. I knew I couldn't let another publisher have it.

My decision to publish Alan Watts' *Touched by Angels* was a result of complete impulsiveness. I just fell in love with it. There is a raw, always-on-edge energy running through the book and the almost Dickensian style of writing is so extraordinarily rare these days, that I knew I couldn't let this live in a desk drawer.

Getting published is tough. Publishing is an industry where everything relies on the ultimate statistics-resistant factor: taste. It's the world of over-excited, over-worked, over-tired, over-hassled people who can only handle a certain amount of books per year. OK, it's over 600,000 in the US and the UK alone, but it is very, very hard for any first-time writer to make it in the top 600,000 and get published.

Approaching independent editors and literary consultants

You should always contact at least an agent before you make the decision to pay for professional help. In fact, an agent's feedback is part of the process of taking this decision. With the right amount of self-editing, it's entirely possible that your work is good enough in the first place and, by approaching an independent editor first, you could waste time and money.

However, this is a two-edged sword. Once you have approached an agent and received a rejection letter, it's highly unlikely that further submissions will be accepted for the same manuscript, regardless of how many revisions it has gone through. That's why many authors, including Harry Bingham, in his excellent guide, *Writers' and Artists' Guide to Getting Published*, advise on getting professional help first before blowing your chances with a highly suitable agent.

The desired middle is to approach an agent first, especially one that offers to give some feedback, and see how your work is received. If it's a rejection, you can then decide whether you wish to approach another agent or get a professional to assess it.

Getting an independent editor or literary consultant to work on your manuscript provides you with an independent and market-aware opinion on the quality and value of your work in the shape of a highly personal and detailed assessment report. Furthermore, if your writing is of outstanding value, a consultant can open the first door for you to a suitable agent of a suitable publisher's editor. Some agents and editors value recommendations from established and recognised literary consultants.

The fact that there is enormous value in an established literary consultant's assessment of a manuscript is a fact the thousands of clients of Daniel Goldsmith Associates and other established literary consultancies can vouch for. You can send us your manuscript for assessment any time. Have a look at www.daniegoldsmith.co.uk for how to proceed.

How to handle criticism of your writing

The only way to handle criticism in every area, not just writing, is to put it to good use. Your best friend has just informed you, 'Your point of view is all over the place.' *Ouch!* It hurts, OK, but what can you do next? Try asking for details. Why? Where? Criticism can be easily turned into a precious resource for improvement.

Some criticism is simply nasty and it needs to be taken with a pinch of salt. You are likely to receive this type of pointless feedback on online forums and so-called 'writing groups', where no one knows anyone and strangers find gratification in insulting other strangers. If you find a particular feedback has been given just for the sake of criticism, i.e. with no arguments and no details, the best thing to do is stop taking notice and move on.

It also makes sense to ensure you're dealing with fair-minded parties when you get feedback on what you write. Especially after best-selling crime author R J Ellory admitted to reviewing positively his own books and very negatively his competitors' on sites such as amazon.co.uk. He wrote on his Facebook page: 'Over the last 10 years I have posted approximately 12 reviews of my own books, and I also criticised a book written by Stuart MacBride, and another by Mark Billingham, both of whom had done nothing to warrant such criticism.' If this happens to you, it's likely to hurt more than the cross-eyed point of view.

As discussed on pages 133–134, Stephen King recognised that bad criticism can be damaging and wrote:

> *I think I was forty before I realized that every writer of fiction and poetry who has ever published a line has been accused by someone of wasting his or her God-given talent. If you write (or paint or dance or sculpt or sing, I suppose), someone will try to make you feel lousy about it, that's all.*
>
> (*On Writing*)

One thing is for sure and that is never shy away from getting feedback on your writing. Feedback is vital and absolutely everyone has an opinion on books, good or bad. Knowing readers' reaction to your scenes, characters, metaphors, etc., is a necessary health check-up for any writer. You never know if your characters are empathic, if your scenes are indeed visual, if you are overwriting or if you have achieved the effect you're after, unless you get feedback from readers.

Is self-publishing a viable option for you?

If you decide to self-publish, you would join a wide company of authors ranging from Beatrix Potter to E.L. James. It's a committing decision, but, done right, it can prove extremely rewarding.

Self-publishing doesn't mean doing all the editorial process all on your own. In fact, responsible and conscious self-publishing will ensure editorial standards are met and this will pay off in the long term, as it will attract readers' respect and increase your book's wow factor. I sometimes receive feedback on my reports from frustrated authors, outraged at being so unfairly misunderstood: 'It's sad to see my point was missed on page 52, paragraph 8. Hannah was in fact pointing out that Jim should have been there and not the other way around.'

This is the point: if one reader missed the point, it's likely that many others will too and you won't know their addresses to send them an erratum on a postcard. That's why feedback at prepress stage is immensely important.

In order to become aware of your book's readiness to reach the published stage, you need some strong feedback from friends and family and professionals, the latter ones being literary agents and professional editors and literary consultants.

You probably wonder why you would need to approach a literary agent with your work if you have already decided to self-publish. It's a legitimate question, the answer being you would be crazy not to. An agent's reaction to your manuscript is a good indicator of its market potential. If the agent comes back with a 'yes, please', you now know there is good potential for success for your book and you should decide what to do next. Either leave it to someone else, i.e. the publisher, to do all the hard work and pay you royalties, or self-publish and try your best and hardest to ensure it achieves success, potentially making you more money.

However, successful self-publishing can also act as a springboard for astonishing mainstream success.

Hugely successful authors such as Cory Doctorow, Amanda Hocking, John Locke and E.L. James all started as self-published authors who got 'fished' by huge publishing houses, often for millions of dollars contracts. Their initial success as self-publishers were firm indicators that, with a powerful marketing and publicity system from a big publisher already in place, they could achieve even higher success. I've always wondered, why do they do it? What kind of value can a publisher add to an author who has a followship of millions? Here's Amanda Hocking's answer, quoted from Forbes.com:

> '*I* only *want to be a writer,*' *Hocking said.* '*I do not want to spend 40 hours a week handling e-mails, formatting covers, finding editors, etc. Right now, being me is a full-time corporation.*'

There are some important questions you need to ask yourself in order to assess whether self-publishing is for you.

Do I have the money to invest in preparing my title for print?

You can't do everything yourself. You write the manuscript, you self-edit it for hours on end, but would you be crazy enough to let it go to print without a professional looking at it first? Professional help here means editorial and prepress services such as development editing, copy-editing, typesetting, proofreading, cover design, illustration as well as printing, if you intend to produce paper books too. If you're looking to publish only digitally, you still need at least a copy-editor and proofreader to ensure quality standards are met.

Do I have the time to promote my book, once published?

Once the book is published, readers need to know about it. There are millions of titles produced every year all over the world, so unless you put in considerable effort, it's likely that very few readers will ever know that it even exists. This can be very disheartening and difficult to accept for many new authors. In giving advice to self-published author Amanda Hocking when she expressed relief at her work being promoted by a publisher instead of by herself only, best-selling author Garth Stein says: 'He who has a thing to sell and goes and whispers in a well, is not as apt to get the dollars as he who climbs a tree and hollers!' (http://www.forbes.com/sites/booked/2011/04/04/advice-for-amanda-hocking-from-authors-and-agents).

Am I comfortable with self-promotion?

This is a biggie. Not everyone likes self-promotion, but self-promotion is a *vital* part of the self-publishing process. You need Facebook and Twitter accounts and every other possible social media channel, at least one blog and endless hours of writing content for the internet with the sole purpose of selling your book. This is immensely time consuming and not necessarily rewarding in the short term. It takes a while for search engines to pick up new content and getting listed high up in search engines is increasingly difficult because everyone seems to be aiming for the same thing.

Besides, it's a known fact that self-promotion is not as efficient as disinterested third-party promotion, so don't forget to count in all the hours you will have to spend trying to build a referral network around you: those influential readers, reviewers and bloggers who find the time to read your book and write about it.

Can you predict a book's success?

I sometimes get asked this question by clients who are trying to make a decision, many of them while waiting for agents and publishers to get back to them. Writers want to know whether their self-published title stands any chance of success and they won't be left with a low bank balance and their garages full of paperbacks.

The truth is that no one can predict the success rate of a fiction book for a new author. Any new author is a gamble and this is by far an understatement. For no reasons at all, some wonderful new books will never take off while others will sell astonishing amounts. *Fifty Shades of Grey* is just of one those inexplicable phenomenona.

Sometimes writers look at sales figures for best-selling titles in their genre and their optimism soars. Unfortunately, this is a vastly misleading direction. If you write like James Patterson, it doesn't mean you will sell well, despite the huge popularity of James Patterson's novels. You would expect that, out of the millions of JP fans, at least half of one per cent would fall for your book. Still, they don't. Why is this? They're quite happy with James Patterson himself and any attempt at matching would come across as second-rate.

For non-fiction titles, predicting is a much easier task and the results are usually closer to reality. No non-fiction editor in their right mind will commission a new title without checking competitors' performance first. The way they do it is by checking sales figures for titles covering the same topic, from best-sellers to poor performers and average them out to get a predicted figure for a strong manuscript.

Nevertheless, anyone can check sales figures for almost any ISBN ever issued by using Nielsen's service, BookScan. So if curiosity gets the better of you, you can contact Nielsen BookScan (www.nielsenbookscan.co.uk) and, for a fee, request their ad-hoc service to check lifetime sale figures in the UK for a particular ISBN.

Conclusion: Self-editing is worth the effort

I hope that by now I don't have to prove this point: self-editing is worth every bit of effort, every minute spent on it.

What is the whole point of self-editing? Creating a superior reading experience for your readers. Immersing them in the universe of your characters. *Immersing* them. The most immersive reading experience is when we lose awareness that we are reading a book. When the narrative flows, the choice of words and atmosphere match the scene so well, we're allowed complete immersion. Complete immersion is when you miss your station because you failed to hear the announcement and you haven't looked out the window in the last ten minutes. Remarkable authors are remarkable because they achieve this effect on their readers.

The bad news is that a lot of self-editing effort needs to be put in for this moment to happen. The good news is that a lot of self-editing effort needs to be put in for this moment to happen. It can happen, but it is up to you. And that's the best bit of news any writer needs.

My personal ability to immerse myself completely in a story as a reader is limited. Having worked as a fiction editor for over 12 years, the way I read fiction is focused not so much on *what*, but on *how*. When I encounter amazing writing, I am mostly interested in how the author does it and what he or she uses to achieve the result. You will find that, the more you self-edit, the more aware of *how they do it* you will become, which can only help you as a fiction writer.

When you're in the editing mindset, something magical happens: you start *reading* fiction in a different way. You become an insightful reader, switching your point of view from *what* to *how*.

Being an active and committed self-editor will make you a better reader, and being both can increase your chances of becoming a significantly better writer. Remember this example:

> Jim trusted the President, not knowing the President was no more than the puppet figure of an oppressive regime.

I said I would come back to it in at the end of the book and there's a good reason why. This is also a perfect example of how you can edit in the synergetic way I mentioned in the introduction. At some point in your self-editing process, you will have gained enough skills to recognise your bad writing to edit with *no* particular filter in mind. This is the point from which editing becomes a mindset and the process gains a certain naturalness about it, a certain easiness that only experienced writers and self-editors share.

As a personal guarantee, there is no great writer in the world that isn't first a great self-editor. Only when your book is published and you receive your first five-star review, you will know that all the effort was worth it.

I hope this book has been the inspiring and motivating start to you becoming a better writer.

Resources

Bingham, H. (2012) *The Writers' and Artists' Guide to How to Write*. A & C Black Publishers.

Brown, R. and King, D. (2004) *Self-Editing for Fiction Writers*. HarperCollins.

Cohen, T. (2011) *The Mistress's Revenge*. Doubleday.

Ephron, H. (2005) *Writing and Selling your Mystery Novel*. Writer's Digest Books.

Dahl, R. (2011) *Danny, the Champion of the World*. Puffin.

Donogue, E. (2010) *Room*. Picador.

Haddon, M. (2004) *The Curious Incident of the Dog in the Night-time*. Vintage.

James, E. L. (2012) *Fifty Shades of Grey*. Arrow.

Kempton, G. (2004) *Dialogue*. Writer's Digest Books.

King, S. (2001) *On Writing*. Hodder & Stoughton.

McInerney, J. (2007) *Bright Lights, Big City*. Bloomsbury.

Newman, S. and Mittelmark, H. (2009) *How Not to Write a Novel*. Penguin.

Obstfeld, R. (2000) *Novelist's Essential Guide to Crafting Scenes*. Writer's Digest Books.

Orwell, G. (2009) *Politics and the English Lanugage*. Penguin Classics.

Palahniuk, C. (1997) *Fight Club*. Vintage.

Poe, E.A. (2009) *Berenice*. Book Surge Classics.

Prado, B. (2006) *Snow is Silent*. Faber and Faber.

Price, J. (2011) *A Means of Escape*. Aston Bay Press.

Price, J. (2012) *Eeny Meeny Miny Moe*. Aston Bay Press.

Prose, F. (2012) *Reading Like a Writer*. Union Books.

Rasley, A. (2008) *The Power of the Point of View*. Writer's Digest.

Ritter, R.M. (2005) *New Hart's Rules*. Oxford University Press.

Sebold, A. (2003) *The Lovely Bones*. Picador.

Strunk Jr, W. and White, E.B. (1999) *The Elements of Style*. Longman.

Watts, N. (2006) *Teach Yourself Writing a Novel*. Hodder Education.

Watts, A. (2012) *Touched by an Angel*. Aston Bay Press.

Writers' and Artists' Yearbook (2012), A & C Black Publishers.

The Writers' and Artists' Yearbook Guide to Getting Published. (2011) A & C Black Publishers.

Zusak, M. (1999) *The Book Thief*. Pan.

Index

abbreviation, 124

abstraction, 53, 82

action, 40, 42, 58, 61, 65, 69–70, 92, 95, 109–11, 115, 121, 149
- consequences (structure), 19–23, 91
  see also escalating conflict

plan, 128, 153

see also alternating action, description and reflection

adjective, 26, 63–4, 66–7, 108

adjectivitis, 63

adverb, 63–7, 72, 74–5

agent, literary *see* literary agent

alternating action, description and reflection, 40–3, 115

Anastasia Steele (character), 87

Angry Robot, 154

Anna Karenina (character), 94

antagonist, 101

see also villain, 2, 14, 19, 86, 97–9

appraisal *see* critique; manuscript assessment

Aquinas, Thomas, 74

Aston Bay Press, 154

atmosphere, 52, 54, 57–9, 63, 72, 102–3, 105–6, 108, 115, 162

see also scene

Atticus Finch (character), 93, 94

audience, 6–7, 41, 60, 77, 85–6, 103, 131, 133, 142, 151

unengaged, 60, 85

Austen, Jane

Pride and Prejudice, 95

backstory, 13, 24, 41, 46–7

Bell, Eddie, 127

Bell, Lomax, Moreton Literary
   Agency, 127
Billingham, Mark, 157
Bingham, Harry, 130, 155, 165
   The Writers' and Artists'
      Yearbook Guide to Getting
      Published, 130, 155
   The Writers' and Artists'
      Yearbook Guide to How to
      Write Better, 165
Book of Mormon, The, 20
Bookseller, The, 132
brackets, 38–9
Brazil, 149–50
Bryant, Mina, xiii
Bulwer-Lytton, Edward George,
   66
   Paul Clifford, 64
   Fiction Contest, 64, 79

Camus, Albert, 93
chapter, 5, 10, 15, 24, 42,
   44–6, 48, 67, 74, 79, 95,
   97, 99, 104, 117, 120, 131,
   140, 144, 152
   break, 47
   mid-, 46, 48
character
   boring, 86
   cardboard, 98
   change, 91–3, 98
   development 91–2

dull, 78, 86–8
edginess, 86, 88
empathy, 85, 91, 93
first-person, 83, 85
   see also narrator
main *see* protagonist
names, 80
overdeveloped, 98–9
random, 88–96
rigid, 91–4
stock, 90, 98
underdeveloped, 97–8
chauvinism, 95–6
Chekhov, Anton, 15, 22, 55
   's Rifle, 15, 22–3, 41, 46,
      89, 103
   see also foreshadowing
chick-lit, 31
children's (genre), 76, 98, 130
Churchill, Julia, 130, 153
clarity, 117–18, 121, 124
cliché, 5, 65, 77–8, 145
cliffhanger, 5, 16, 24, 42, 44–8
   mid-chapter, 46
   end of chapter, 45
Cohen, Tamar
   The Mistress's Revenge, 29
Coleridge, Gill, 138
Collins, Jackie, 144
comedy, 91
Comedia dell'Arte, 91
conflict, 2, 5, 13–21, 41–2, 87

escalating, 5, 14, 18–19, 41

confusion, 32–3

  see also observation –
    perception

consistency, 10, 37, 117–18,
  120

consultant, literary *see* literary
  consultant

copyright, 118

Coronation Street, 8

covering letter, 138–9, 142–6,
  151–3

creative writing, 2, 8–9, 19, 69,
  76

critique *see* appraisal;
  manuscript assessment

Daniel Goldsmith Associates,
  xiii, 44, 120, 128, 156

debut, 132–3

defamation, 118

dénouement, 15, 44, 92

  see also ending

description, 4, 15, 40, 42, 54,
  57, 61, 67, 81, 85, 106,
  112–13, 115, 136, 145, 148

block, 42, 57, 81

  see also alternating action,
    description and reflection

Deus ex Machina, 17, 89

dialogue, 37, 43–5, 56, 59,
  68–74, 78, 83, 89, 97, 99,

102, 123–4

  vivid, 68, 72, 123

diary entries, 19

Dickensian (style), 154

Doctorow, Cory, 159

Donoghue, Emma

  Room, 31, 87

  Jack (narrator), 31–2, 87

edge, 86–8

editing

  as mindset, 3–4, 8, 10, 163

  synergetic, 10, 56, 163

editor

  copy-, 117–18, 124, 159

  development, 117

  independent, 129, 133–4,
    155

    see also literary consultant

  self-, 4, 33, 67, 105, 163

Ellroy, R.J., 156

ending

  alternative, 6

  necessary, 18

  satisfying, 18, 151

Enright, Anne, 137–8

Eugenides, Jeffrey

  The Virgin Suicides, 27–8

ExhibitA, 154

explaining, 54, 74–7

  see also overwriting

exposition, 19, 58–9

Facebook, 93, 157, 160
fair use, 118
fantasy, 14, 51, 80, 91, 110, 111
fiction
  new, 27, 127, 132, 133
  unedited, 5, 50
  unpublished, 50
  -writing, 27, 28, 49, 50, 53,
    60, 65, 79
first-person narrator, 27–31,
  39, 82, 83, 85, 108
focus (of a scene), 43, 103–4
Forbes.com, 159
foreshadowing, 22
  see also Chekhov's Rifle

genre fiction, 2, 6, 7, 8, 12,
  161
grammar, 118, 119, 121, 122,
  139
Green, Katie, xiii, 139
Guardian, The, 132

Hardy, Thomas, 45
Hocking, Amanda, 159–60
Holden Caulfield (character),
  93–4
Hollinghurst, Alan, 15
Homer, 17, 79
  Ulysses, 79
homophones, 123

Horace, 17
horror, 31, 36, 80
Huffington Post, 132
HuffPost Books, 93
Hurst, Andrea, 19

inconsistency, 33, 37, 56, 92,
  128
intimacy, 30–1, 39, 54
Ishmael (character), 6

James, E.L., 157, 159
Jay Gatsby (character), 93
Johns, Jasper, 49
Joyce, James
  Ulysses, 79
Julie Capulet (character), 94

King, Stephen, 66, 134, 157
  On Writing, 133, 157

LGBT, 142
literary agent, 1, 19, 116,
  127–37, 146, 158
literary consultant, 1, 2, 3, 5,
  27, 96, 110, 117, 129, 133,
  134, 136, 155–6, 158
  see also independent editor
Locke, John, 159
London Book Fair, 127
Luck, Lucy, 138

manuscript
    assessment, 13, 16, 27, 42,
        117, 155, 156
        see also appraisal; critique
    market, 2, 7, 131, 132, 133,
        138, 152, 158
    -awareness, 129, 133, 155
    insight, 11
    value, 5
McBride, Stuart, 157
McInerney, Jay
    Bright Lights, Big City, 29
Melville, Herman, 6
mirror, 82–3, 102–3
mistake, 5, 35, 38, 121, 122,
    140
Mr Bennet (character), 95
Munch, Edvard
    The Scream, 62

narration, 26, 30, 72
narrative, 3, 4, 5, 6, 11, 26, 28,
    29, 30, 32, 37, 38, 39, 42,
    45, 51, 56, 66, 69, 99, 105,
    107, 108, 117, 123, 162
narrator
    alternating, 31, 32
    first-person, 29–31
    horizontal, 28
    multiple, 31
    objective, 28, 31
    omniscient, 28, 56

subjective, 28, 32, 36, 56,
    108
third-person, 30–1, 39, 85
unreliable, 29, 31
vertical, 28
new books *see* debut
New York Review of Books, The,
    132
Newton, Isaac, 20
Nielsen BookScan, 162
nod-off, 17
non-fiction, 3, 39, 117, 118,
    120, 135, 153, 161

observation – perception, 32–3
Obstfeld, Raymond
    *Novelist's Essential Guide to
        Crafting Scenes*, 67
Ockham
    's Razor, 68, 75
    William, 68
optical affiliation, 36
Orwell, George
    *Politics and the English
        Language*, 50
overwriting, 74–7
    see also explaining
Oxford Dictionary of English,
    105

Palahniuk, Chuck
    Fight Club, 29

Parker, Trey, 20
Patterson, James, 25, 41, 46,
    161
perspective, 26–31, 33, 35–7,
    39, 43, 47, 51, 87, 91, 144
Pi Patel (character), 93, 94
Picoult, Jodi, 69
plot
    multi-, 46
    multi-layered, 45, 47
Poe, E. A., 108
    Berenice, 29, 108
point of view, 4, 6, 10, 26,
    27–8, 30–7, 47, 51, 56, 78,
    80, 156–7, 163
    alternating, 32
Popescu, Simona
    Exuviae, 93
pornography, 3, 36
Potter, Beatrix, 157
Prado, Benjanim
    Snow is Silent, 30, 31
Price, Joanna, 154
    A Means of Escape, 95
    Eeny, Meeny, Miny Moe, 15
proof, 119–20
    -reader, 116, 119–20, 159
    -reading, 119, 159
Prose, Francine
    Reading like a Writer, 104
protagonist, 2, 13–16, 18–19,
    27, 30, 40–2, 84, 85, 86,

88–90, 97, 101, 111, 143
publisher, 116, 119–20, 124,
    128–9, 132–4, 136, 144,
    146, 153–4, 156, 158–61
    self-, 159
Publishers Lunch, 132
Publishers Marketplace, 132
Publishers Weekly, 132
publishing, 2, 120, 127–9, 154
    house, 120
    self-, 5, 157–60
punctuation, 67, 74, 118, 119,
    121, 124
purpose, 8, 32, 67, 70, 85, 90,
    98, 99, 104, 113, 115, 118,
    147, 160
    – focus test, 103–4

randomness, 16, 22, 92
Rasley, Alicia
    The Power of Point of View,
    34
reader, 34, 38–45, 47, 49,
    52–3, 55–7, 59–60, 65,
    69–71, 73–6, 80–2, 84–8,
    90–3, 95–6, 98–105, 107–8,
    111–15, 124, 126, 128, 132,
    141–2, 147, 151, 154,
    157–8, 160, 162–3
    see also audience
red herring, 15, 23
Rees, Emlyn, 154

reflection, 40, 42, 115
  see also alternating action,
    description and reflection
report
  assessment, 96, 117, 155,
    158
  -writing, 56, 60,
    see also witness report
Rogers, Coleridge and White,
  138
rule, 5, 8–10, 12, 50, 120

scene, 4, 11, 14–16, 20, 22,
  34–7, 42–8, 52, 54–5, 57–9,
  62–4, 67, 82, 91, 93, 100,
  102–8, 111–15, 117, 119,
  157, 162
  visual, 37, 54–5, 157
  see also atmosphere
sci-fi, 14, 51, 111, 134
Scotland Yard, 149
Sebold, Alice
  The Lovely Bones, 30
senses, 55
sequel, 19, 145, 149, 151
  trap, 19, 25
setting, 40, 47, 103, 106,
  108–9, 111–15, 117–19
Shakespeare, 142
short story, 2, 7, 9, 96, 104,
  118, 131, 134
showing, 10, 38, 39, 50–63,

67, 70, 75, 78, 81–2, 85,
  95, 102, 111
South Park, 20
state of being, 61–2
Stein, Garth, 160
Stone, Matt, 20
storytelling, 1, 26
Strunk and White, 109
  Elements of Style, 64, 103,
    108
summarisation, 20, 52, 57–9,
  81, 95
suspense, 5, 16, 31, 42, 47
Switzerland, 149
synopsis, 13, 25, 135, 138,
  142, 143, 147–51

Telfer, Jonathan, xiii
telling, 10, 38–9, 50–1, 53,
  55–63, 67, 70, 73, 75, 78,
  81–2, 85, 102, 104, 111
thinking
  creative, 3–4
  critical, 3–4
thriller, 2, 6, 31, 39, 40, 41,
  45, 46, 137, 149, 150
  corporate, 148
  fantasy, 99
  military, 40
  political, 40
  psychological, 31
  sci-fi, 51

social, 40
techno-, 14, 40
Times Literary Supplement, The,
132
tippi fissi, 91
Twitter, 160
Tyler Durden (character), 29

value
artistic, 49
market, 5
verb
precise, 64
Victor Hazell (character), 98
villain, 2, 14, 19, 86, 97–9
see also antagonist
voice, 26–7, 31–2, 60, 74, 153

Watts, Alan
Touched by Angels, 33, 105,
154
widows and orphans, 119
Wikipedia, 26, 95
witness report, 60, 110

see also report-writing
word choice, 26, 32, 79, 103–7
word picture, 54–5, 57
workshop, 1, 9, 20, 25, 128–9
writer, 30, 34, 37, 42–3, 45,
49, 52–3, 66, 68–9, 75,
85–7, 91, 93, 119, 127–30,
134–6, 144, 147, 152–3,
155, 157, 159, 161–3
first-time-, 69, 86, 92, 97,
155
Writers' and Artists' Yearbook,
136, 146, 151
Writer's Digest, 132
Writers' Forum, 132
Writers' Workshop, 129
writing
creative, 2, 8–9, 19, 69, 76
new, 1, 15, 54, 74, 88, 102,
104, 112, 122
Writing Magazine, xiii, 9, 132

Zusak, Markus
The Book Thief, 30

Some other titles from How To Books

365 WAYS TO GET YOU WRITING
Inspiration and advice for creative writers on a daily basis
JANE COOPER

This book will bring you a year's advice and inspiration to move your writing forward on a regular basis. Each two-page spread opens with learning points and advice, followed by interesting exercises to help you create believable characters; write realistic dialogue; improve your writing through reading; use personal experience to inspire fiction; find the factors that get a story going; choose the right tense and person for your stories; show, rather than tell; and work out which writing rules really matter – and follow them.

ISBN 978-1-84528-461-8

HOW TO WRITE EROTIC FICTION AND SEX SCENES
Ashley Lister

This indispensable guide is for anyone wanting to include compelling, well-crafted and saleable sex scenes within their fiction.

With information on preferred vocabulary, the limitations of the genre, erotic characters, sex-positive writing, and literary erotica, this book demonstrates some of the most effective ways that convincing sex scenes can be portrayed on the page. It uses examples from a broad range of writers, and exercises that have been tested successfully in workshops and classrooms throughout the country.

ISBN 978-1-84528-505-0

100 WAYS TO PUBLISH AND SELL YOUR OWN E-BOOK... *AND MAKE IT A BESTSELLER*
Conrad Jones & Darin Jewell

If you've published an e-book, or are planning to do so, this essential guide provides expert advice on every step of the process, from production through to all-important promotion.

This book will give show you how you can give your e-book the best chance of reaching its intended audience, through cover design and formatting, by understanding your options in terms of publishing platforms, pricing and promoting it appropriately and knowing which social networking, bookmarking and cataloguing sites are best suited to showcase it.

ISBN: 978-1-84528-507-4

MORE FIVE-MINUTE WRITING
Another 50 inspiring exercises in creative writing in five minutes a day
Margret Geraghty

From the author of our bestselling *The Five Minute Writer* come 50 more inspirational exercises to inspire you to write – even if you have only five minutes a day to spare.

In this book Margret Geraghty includes a new feature: snippet triggers, which she has designed to show readers how they can develop quirky little anecdotes they find in newspapers, and regional broadcasts. Her daily warm-up exercises will help you to: develop a reliable and enjoyable writing routine, break through the dreaded writing block, open your mind, step out of your comfort zone and set free your creative thought, access your inner self and the personal memories that provide an inexhaustible source of story ideas.

ISBN 978-1-84528-509-8

Write or phone for a catalogue to:

How To Books
Spring Hill House
Spring Hill Road
Begbroke
Oxford
OX5 1RX
Tel. 01865 375794

Or email: info@howtobooks.co.uk

Visit our website www.howtobooks.co.uk to find out more about us and
our books.

Like our Facebook page How To Books & Spring Hill

Follow us on Twitter @Howtobooksltd

Read our books online www.howto.co.uk